Relax on Impact

One of the greatest challenges of substance use disorder treatment is understanding the impact this disease has on the family and assisting them to recognize this impact, confront this impact, and heal from this impact in a nonjudgmental and nurturing way. Jill Haire has taken all of her experience, strength, and hope and embodied it into an entertaining, educating, and inspirational story about addiction, dysfunction, surrender, and transformation. Through powerful symbols and images of the life journey of a "Perfect Cloud," we are able to begin our own journey into acceptance and healing, arriving at a new healthier place where the chains of generational dysfunction no longer enslave our future.

—**Tim Huckaby, MD**
Medical Director of the Orlando Recovery Center
President of the Florida Society of Addiction Medicine
Board-Certified physician in pain medicine,
addiction medicine, and anesthesiology

The protagonist in this novel, the cloud, starts out as Perfect Cloud but takes on various other names as her journey progresses on Earth. "Relax on Impact" is a lesson she takes with her from heaven, on a conscious level, and she uses it when faced with danger. The very act of that relaxation opens up a portal for her, and she is given directions as to how to heal herself and regain single vision once again. She realizes that the love and caring she accepted as her natural birthright had always been there for her; it had never gone away.

The primary purpose of this book is to explore the effect of addictions on the family. To this end, the author chooses the family prototype mentioned above to illustrate exactly what happens to most people when old family patterns are repeated across generations, and how they reinforce themselves over time. I recommend this unusual book very strongly to all, but especially to those battling with addictions and acceptance issues.

—**Bani Sodermark, PhD**
Professor of mathematical physics and mathematics
(university level) in both India and Sweden

Relax on Impact is a clever story of the slide into the abyss of self-will and the courageous journey back to the true self. It will provide both entertainment and insight as you follow the tumultuous journey that leads to the ultimate destination.

—**Charlene Sears-Tolbert**
Certified Addictions Professional and
international board-certified addictions counselor
Director, Auburndale Bridge Residential
Substance Abuse Treatment Program
Author, *When Relationships Hurt—52 Ways to Heal*

Relax On Impact is a cleverly written tale about a journey to wholeness through the storms of life. This is a deep but easy read that will have you laughing out loud, nodding your head, and turning the page to see what happens next.

—**Stephanie Preston, M.Ed**
University of Central Florida
Licensed Mental Health Counselor, National Certified Counselor

A divinely inspired and very powerful parable about a soul's journey from and return to God. The author's use of the parable and unique names takes the reader out of their intellect and allows the message to be received in a subtle but powerful way. I recommend this book for anyone on an emotional and spiritual journey (which is everyone) as it shows that we must become an emotional adult before we can come back to recognition of our spiritual relationship with God.

—**Lawrence Doochin,**
Author, *To Everything There Is a Season*

Relax
on Impact

Transformation and Empowerment
Through Surrender

Jill Haire

NEW YORK

NASHVILLE MELBOURNE

Relax on Impact
Transformation and Empowerment Through Surrender

© 2017 **Jill Haire**

Published in New York, New York, by Morgan James Publishing. Morgan James and The Entrepreneurial Publisher are trademarks of Morgan James, LLC. www.MorganJamesPublishing.com

The Morgan James Speakers Group can bring authors to your live event. For more information or to book an event visit The Morgan James Speakers Group at www.TheMorganJamesSpeakersGroup.com.

Shelfie

A **free** eBook edition is available with the purchase of this print book.

CLEARLY PRINT YOUR NAME ABOVE IN UPPER CASE

Instructions to claim your free eBook edition:
1. Download the Shelfie app for Android or iOS
2. Write your name in **UPPER CASE** above
3. Use the Shelfie app to submit a photo
4. Download your eBook to any device

ISBN 978-1-68350-046-9 paperback
ISBN 978-1-68350-047-6 eBook
ISBN 978-1-68350-048-3 hardcover
Library of Congress Control Number:
2016906107

Cover Design by:
John Weber

Interior Design by:
Bonnie Bushman
The Whole Caboodle Graphic Design

In an effort to support local communities, raise awareness and funds, Morgan James Publishing donates a percentage of all book sales for the life of each book to Habitat for Humanity Peninsula and Greater Williamsburg.

Get involved today! Visit
www.MorganJamesBuilds.com

Contents

Foreword

As a voracious reader, I love reading many different genres of literature, from history to more modern day works. Through my years of medical school as well as psychiatric residency I have also read a considerable number of self-help books. This helped me keep up with what my patients might be reading as well as give me some useful suggestions for reading for them and their families.

When I heard about Jill's book, Relax on Impact, I was intrigued. Having served as the Medical Director of a residential drug treatment facility and served as the Chief of Psychiatry at various hospitals, I have treated many patients suffering from addictions, including alcohol. I have seen the emotional suffering experienced by their families. I wanted to learn more about this book which seemed to offer solutions to practitioners, patients and their loved ones.

Relax on Impact is a powerful story reflecting many parts of the author's life, told in allegorical form and illustrated through various weather formations. I was entertained as I followed the central character named Perfect Cloud as she spiraled in a self-willed trek to her new home, Earth. As I read all about her life's journeys, I didn't want to put the book down. It reminds me of The Shack, as it reveals a powerful spiritual message that provides the hope and healing for those who are truly seeking relief.

As a visionary person myself, I can relate to Jill's vision for people in recovery and their families. When I founded La Amistad, I started with the same thought process. I saw a group of patients with a specific need and knew I needed to do everything I could to see this need met. We started with a twelve bed facility which has grown to date to 280 beds in five different locations.

Jill Haire has a big vision as well. She turns life stories into real tools that can lead to resolution in the lives of people suffering from the torment of addictions, whether from drugs and alcohol, relationships and/or codependency. Her approach is fresh, it is entertaining, educational and inspiring. Most of all, she has walked the walk. She teaches emotional literacy and shows the reader what the process of letting go entails. It is my hope that the reader and those they love will find help through the book, Relax on Impact, as well as from the subsequent programs that will be its offspring.

Walter J. (Joe) Muller, MD
Emory University School of Medicine, Emory, Georgia
Chief Resident and Clinical Instructor, Cornell Medical College, Westchester, New York
Founder of La Amistad Residential Treatment Center, Maitland, Florida

Preface

On September 30, 1999, I had been in substance addiction recovery for two years. In many ways my life had been saved. My next issue was relationship addiction. During that deeper journey, my entire life was challenged while on the road. I was traveling at fifty miles per hour when another car pulled out in front of me just as I came to an intersection. With no time to hit the brakes or turn the wheel, I realized I couldn't control anything and was about to die. I silently surrendered my life and turned my head.

Then a voice I had never heard before, with a message I had never known, spoke to me clearly. It came from somewhere deep in my chest, saying, "Let go. Relax on impact."

I put my head down on the steering wheel and closed my eyes. The cars crashed at full force. I thought I had died. Instead, when I lifted my head, I saw that the car was demolished but I was unharmed.

The other driver's car was totaled too. I later learned that she had just been released from a hospital and was heavily medicated. She had "relaxed on impact" quite easily. She was also unharmed.

The message I heard stayed with me and became the inspiration for this book. Along the way I earned the credentials of Licensed Mental Health Counselor, National Certified Counselor, and Certified Addictions Professional.

After counseling people in a residential treatment facility, I worked with the terminally ill in a hospice organization. I learned how to confront; I learned how to comfort. I learned to help some people let go and fall into what we call "death." I learned to counsel others in how to hold on and build something new, right where they were. I learned to support still others as they made decisions to leave—rather than run away from—situations that weren't becoming healthy and probably never would.

My private practice, Free Flow Counseling, is located in Orlando, Florida. I bring skills and offer guidance to those who are willing to become aware and empowered. Through Free Flow Consulting I provide professional education, keynote speaking, and consulting services for providers and organizations.

Relax on Impact brings the reader through a difficult journey many of us share. Well-meaning, imperfect parents offer imperfect love. Insecurity from faulty connection with parents creates needs that continue into adulthood. Addictions, power struggles, and emotional unavailability build anger walls meant to protect the child. Each generation seems doomed to teach past mistakes.

Marriages built between disempowered individuals seeking their "other half" create repeated divorces and added pain instead of increased intimacy, love, and spiritual clarity. This codependency, also known as relationship addiction, affects most of us to some degree.

Expressed in parable form, *Relax on Impact* tells the story of Perfect Cloud, who leaves her original perfect home. She confuses the new Imperfect Love of Earth parents with the Perfect Love she's always known. She transforms into simply Cloud. Her name continues to change in response to her thoughts, her feelings, and then her physical appearance. She eventually becomes the powerful HerACane. Her descent into the tornadic winds of addiction and dysfunction, however, drops her from Power Full to Power Fall.

The obliteration she has always feared seems imminent. However, that final drop reveals a brand-new name. Surrender, transformation, and empowerment lead her to freedom.

Relax on Impact is designed to entertain, educate, and inspire. It is my hope that you will also come to hear the clear small voice that I heard during the car crash, and that saved my life. In *Relax on Impact* I refer to that voice as EYE M, the presence that is always with us.

May your journey bring you the peace and understanding that you seek. And so it is.

Chapter 1
Bliss Full and Bliss Fall

♥ ♥ ♥ ♥ ♥

Do you remember your first love? Before you were ever born, you knew bliss far greater than any Earth love could ever be. You were perfect and perfectly loved. Your Perfect Vision, compliments of EYE M Higher Power, created joy within you and all around you. In a weak moment, you chose to separate from this love. The Impostars called your name. You followed. You became Earthbound. This life began. Perfect Cloud takes us on her journey that begins with leaving EYE Will to explore Self-Will. Much of her life is symbolic for us all.

E YE M was Perfect Love. He was also Perfect Cloud's perfect parent. For as long as she could remember, Perfect Cloud knew a Bliss Full existence with EYE M. Connected, elevated, and supported high in the sky, she basked in the warmth and comfort of His love. Centered in the sun by day, she felt His special light shining down on her. At day's end He painted sunsets in neon pinks and vivid purples, for He knew those were her favorite colors. Centered in the moon by night, she gazed at the vibrant yellow ball high against the navy curtained sky that served as her night-light. Centered in sweetness, she fed continuously on the warm love He knew she craved.

He directed this nourishment into the rosy, contented heart center that she always offered up to Him. Her fluffy layers glowed pink with love overflow. He energized her movements with lightning tickles and fizzles. She flowed freely, without effort. She allowed and trusted EYE M's Perfect Vision and Perfect Hearing to see and hear for her. She witnessed the multicolored beauty of the world around her. She heard dimensional music with magical, resonating tones that surrounded her soul, a perfect match for Perfect Love. Their shared theme song served as a consistent foundational melody. He supplied endless variations from added styles. Life was perfect.

EYE M knew her in all ways, inside and out. He had a perfect plan made just for her life, called EYE Will. Saturated and secure, Perfect Cloud sang songs radiating from her full, satisfied heart and moved with uninhibited joy to the rhythm of her pulsing inner beat—her very own drums! She trusted that every time she somersaulted down into the empty sky, EYE M's unfailing support would catch her before she fell too far. She opened her mouth as laughter bubbled up, overflowed, and burst out, blowing rays of sheer delight out into the heavens.

Perfect Cloud. Even her name flowed. The sky's blue deepened. She smiled, reaching out to touch birds and butterflies. They responded by resting on her, flowing through her, or drifting alongside her. Their energy reflected and returned the Perfect Love inside of her.

Wherever she went, EYE M was all around her. His fleecy warmth conveyed a love force so large she couldn't see past it and didn't want to try. He knew where she wanted to go even when she didn't know for sure herself!

One unusual day Perfect Cloud's attention wavered. She drifted a little farther away than usual. EYE M watched her closely. She tilted herself forward ever so slightly and noticed that her movement increased. Her awareness changed. The contrast! Many spotlights appeared. They hooked her attention and then captured it by pointing in all different directions. Her natural, free-flowing movement jerked and stopped altogether. The glare was intense. Her new outward focus placed Perfect Vision on pause, and in a moment it clouded over.

Perfect Cloud was blinded. Then something popped up on the outside of her face. She blinked and refocused with new My Sight. Her view widened and lengthened. She had somehow created an illusion, and now she could see intriguing formations. This My Sight, also known as Earth Vision, revealed details of a world she had never noticed, spread out in all different shapes. Just above it, new stars beckoned by night with winks and twinkles. The longer she stared at them and listened to their calls, the more appealing they became.

A humming sound within her grew louder and louder. A spurt of intense, personal desire Perfect Cloud had never felt surged through her. This force, called My Will Power, caused her to further detach from EYE Will. It also strengthened My Sight. She pressed out a forceful, final jolt of My Will Power that caused a second My Sight to pop out on the other side of her face. My Sight was now replaced with even more concentrated *Double* My Sight. She had achieved Double Vision!

She clapped with delight at My Will Power, but for some reason she also shivered. Her form responded to this energy by moving in a circle to the right. As she thought back for a moment to EYE Will and Perfect Love, she moved in a circle to the left and felt a little dizzy.

At the same moment, EYE M Ear sounds became muffled and then she was deaf. An appendage popped out on the side of her head.

Cupping her hand behind this new My Ear, she listened intently. Sounds widened from beyond her in a way she had never heard, and her single My Ear was replaced with Double Hearing! The music sounded strange now, with discordant overtones. The beat seemed to drum from outside of her.

My Sight focused on layers of stars that flashed and sparkled. One seemed to be the brightest, glittering with the promise of an ever-changing display. In contrast, EYE M's Star stood alone—neither shiny nor flashy. Its light was steady and unchanging.

Perfect Cloud switched her gaze to the brighter star and then turned briefly toward EYE M.

"Wow, look! Listen! New music and exciting, sparkly stars! I want to go there," she told Him, pointing down to an overly shiny group of star attachments. "IMP Stars! They must be important," Perfect Cloud added in a hushed voice.

"They're Impostars," corrected EYE M as He studied her gaze. "Imperfect Love. They're all empty. It's best to stay here and be entertained from afar."

Perfect Cloud turned away from Him, smiled confidently, and shook her head. "No, they're not empty. Look at what I see with My Sight. Listen to what I hear with My Ear." She pointed to three of the largest in the group. "All of them are more, more, more! They're telling me their names: Power, Resources, and So Much More Love!"

As she watched their light show, a jolt shot through her center, far greater than EYE M's gentle sizzles. "They're beautiful. Heavenly, even! I want to be with them. I might even plug into them for a while."

EYE M shared her vision in silence. Then He asked, "Shall EYE come too?"

"No. I want to go all by myself," she stated with conviction. She pulled as far away as possible from EYE M's connection. The connector cables stretched and became taut. Perfect Cloud tugged harder, almost harming herself in the process. "I can do it alone with My Will Power!"

For the first time ever, she decided that EYE Will and My Will were not the same.

EYE M, centered in the sun, observed her. He allowed her release. She unplugged, cable attachments dangling. Freedom! His winds blew softly to support her journey of independent movement.

Puffing up and leaning forward, Perfect Cloud sailed away from Him on the winds He provided. For a while she enjoyed the ride, but gradually the warmth from EYE M faded. Bliss Fall was on its way. The beautiful colors around her vanished. The music from within her diminished and then stopped. The music outside of her disappeared. The silence roared, threatening her with unknown dangers. She stared through My Sight at purples and pinks that intensified and faded into a fiery sunset. She searched the sky as darkness blanketed her. No yellow ball rose high up to light the darkness of her night. She expressed a surge of My Will Power to fly even faster.

At last she was depleted. Her movement paused and then stopped. Her course reversed abruptly when a magnetic pull from behind and below jerked her backward. Unable to see from this position, she heard the resurgent moan of discordant music as she fell.

Trailing the remains of spectacular, feathered clouds of glory, she plummeted into the sky—down, down, down. Tornadic winds whipped her, pounding into her two sensitive My Ears. As she dropped lower, each Impostar called out in a loud voice. She longed for EYE M's quiet voice and reassuring light. Her pink-tinged layers emptied. Once again she faced the massive layers of Earth that seemed to expand by the second. My Sight revealed dark places hidden beneath it all. She shuddered and desperately wrapped herself within her own folds for protection.

"Wherever You are, Perfect Love, please help me!" she begged aloud.

Instantly a calming, blue light from EYE M's Star appeared, named R.O.I., Relax on Impact. And once again everything seemed safe and familiar. She relaxed into the warm soft light and onto a blue butterfly that emerged out of nowhere to support her journey home again.

Even the faint beams of starlight leading back to EYE M's Perfect Love refueled her pale heart with a pink and purple flush. Her vision and hearing changed back to their original perfection, and she was carried along without a struggle. Perfect Love re-nourished her heart and re-strengthened it with courageous purple.

In a flash, she redirected this energy to refuel My Will Power. Her focus immediately shifted. When a single white spotlight appeared from lower in the darkening blue sky, her attention centered on two large bright stars near Earth. Her sight and hearing returned to My Sight. She had used up My Will Power, borrowed EYE M's Star Power, and used it to leave Him—again.

At that moment Perfect Cloud shook her head and made a decision. She would totally reconnect herself, all right, but not to EYE M. She would visit Earth—now. She would replace EYE M, EYE Will, and EYE Will Power with Me, My Will, and My Will Power. It would be different this time. She would direct her own life and become more and more powerful until she was no longer a cloud at all but a FORCE backed by a wondrous star of her own! What a celebration she would have!

The butterfly sensed her thought and released her. She floated toward Earth. Bliss Fall increased.

Quickly and quietly an unknown figure arrived, created an opening for her in Earth, and disappeared. Perfect Cloud felt Power Full as colors changed around her. She reconnected her magically updated cables quite easily into the Earth keyhole. The glare from one star was so bright at close range that Perfect Cloud had to close My Sight altogether. She grabbed a pair of My Sun glasses that appeared out of nowhere and was able to see clearly. The world down near Earth looked gray and forbidding. From just below, two stars reached up to offer her a pair of My Rose-Colored glasses. She dropped the My Sun glasses to slip these on. Through their muted, flushed coating, her outer vision reopened to see the Earth in a different way, the pure fantasy known as Earth Pink I. Denial. Bliss Full!

These stars, called "parents," used her new name, simply Cloud. The word "Perfect" had disappeared. Cloud felt a twinge deep inside and promised herself she'd earn back that word "Perfect" from the Impostars, no matter how long it took.

The star parents merged into one light and held her close. She surrendered to each of them. Their combined energy permeated her suddenly empty heart. Their light was very bright, even brighter than EYE M's had been. It flickered, though, and sometimes felt cool, unlike the consistent warmth of EYE M. Still, the result was much the same as her heart softened, melted, and opened. She tried to return the My Rose-Colored glasses, but the stars motioned her to tuck them into her folds, just in case she ever needed them again. They even gave her an extra, stronger pair.

Until now Cloud had never known what "empty" or "hungry" meant, but she learned fast. She quickly learned to rely upon Mom and Dad, who took turns trying repeatedly to fill her heart.

Her first substitute nourishment came directly from Mother Cloud, and then from a bottle. Both were different from EYE M's. This nourishment was white, not pink, and only slightly sweet. Eventually Mother and Daddy Cloud fed her other food with a spoon. This sustenance seemed to fill her briefly, but she always needed more, desperately!

Sobbing, she inflamed inside and out in an effort to get their attention. She reached up into the air, panicking and shaking. When that failed, she screamed and waved angry fists. When even that didn't produce results, she contracted herself into a ball. Eventually they returned. Her heart full, she relaxed again, but it didn't last. With this Imperfect Love she alternately felt lost, abandoned, and hopeless, followed by peaceful, warm, and protected—until she felt empty again. The cycle of inconsistency repeated itself until she renamed the process and her parents Perfect Love.

Suddenly, wondrous music returned from far away. EYE M Ear opened, but only for a few seconds. Unanswered, the music faded and disappeared.

Cloud studied her new world through heart-shaped My Sight glasses that floated by. At last she fell—fell in love with Earth. She descended into a deep, deep sleep.

Chapter 2
Play Full And Play Fall

Cloud finds herself in a new version of security. She lives in a bubble with Mother Cloud and Daddy. He has increased in size to a Double HimACane and has much more power than before. Cloud is taught to trust him with all her heart and learns to "play small" for his approval. When he drinks something called Toxic Rain from a strange-looking cloud, his personality changes. Cloud's life begins to change, too.

When Cloud awakened she was settled into a small house that was *just the right size.* Daddy HimACane whirled around to produce *just enough* Debris Resources for them all.

But each night darkness descended and emptiness seeped into her center. Her My Sight blurred. Her gaze slowly moved upward and landed on a special star that was steady and clear. It had a name she couldn't read. But when she switched her focus back to Earth and then up again, the special star blurred.

"Someday," Cloud whispered. "Someday I'll travel to that beautiful star *all by myself*—with My Will and My Will Power!"

Her empty heart caused her to rain and wail in pain. Mother Cloud directed her mild light into the area. Daddy HimACane topped it off with heated energy that lingered. Now Cloud could sleep, but Mother Cloud's excited voice interrupted her dreams.

"Wake up, sweet Cloud! Look at Daddy—he's become a Double HimACane! His powerful double winds stirred up massive amounts of Debris Resources, and I'm off to collect them all. At last we can have anything we want! We'll live in a huge new home too!"

Mother Cloud beamed up at Daddy, who posed proudly. He had now doubled in size and power, his dual, rotating energies lifted high.

Cloud clapped her hands, but for some reason she also shivered. She drifted off into confusing dreams.

When she awoke she remembered she had a new, larger status from many more Resources. Intense energy swelled and filled her heart space, increasing her size and lifting her higher in the sky. She unfurled her feathered edges as Daddy approached. Just behind him stood Mother Cloud, decorated with festive coverings and colorful accents that only partially hid her gray heart center with its long Ice Train. As always, she attached herself to Daddy when she could.

When Mother took Cloud *outside* their bubble home alone, she trailed behind her child. From this unusual maternal posture she used her Afraid Are screen to scan the sky and the Earth below for any dangers. Helplessly immobile herself, Mother Cloud always summoned her mate in such a case. He'd be there in an instant with his massive circular winds to protect Cloud.

When all three of them were safely *within* their bubble home, Daddy entertained them with elegant, classical Boxed Music. Mother Cloud simply polished her instrument, hid it in her folds, and listened. Cloud clapped to the music, listening for her own inner beat. Daddy's timing from the practice clicker was so loud it overpowered hers. She told herself she could borrow Daddy Double HimACane's beat; it was all she really needed.

Ah, then there was Play Fall, the private game that she and Daddy played together. Mother only watched as Cloud flapped her tiny cirrus wings to climb up the My Fall Tower. Daddy watched and waited until, on cue, Cloud slid down a steep incline. She fell into empty air pockets from which they all knew she could not escape.

Ta-da! Daddy was there, as always, to rescue her. Cloud laughed and clung to him with gratitude as Daddy checked Mother Cloud's reaction. When she smiled and nodded, Daddy beamed and once again invited Cloud to Play Fall.

One day Cloud's attention wandered to an ivory seagull in flight. Spotting a wind gust, she floated over to hitch a ride. She jumped off and flipped onto her stomach to coast alongside the unsuspecting gull. When it changed course in alarm, she guided herself to match its path. She closed in on her target, reaching out with cottony hands to grab onto the bird with all her might. Unfazed, it flew straight through her inner layers and out the other side, leaving droppings on her head.

Cloud darkened all over. Her belly swelled and reddened. Then she exploded into a sobbing, little storm of tiny, circular winds and torrential rain.

Mother Cloud first assessed the response of passing weather forms. One or two gave her a long hot look, frowned, and shook their heads. She reddened and shrank, thrusting assorted Pacify Hers toward Cloud. Cloud turned her head, refusing the tokens. Mother turned her own head, lifted it high, and inhaled a Dust Devil Tube.

That sudden, uncensored heat reaction burned, adding to the smoke surrounding Cloud. She opened her downturned mouth in a wide wail. Mother Cloud withdrew altogether and frantically waved for help.

Daddy Double HimACane screeched to Cloud's side. Cupping her pale face with his soothing, outermost breezes, he blew away her tears, drawing her through his massive winds into the peace within one of his small, well-defined My Sights. Relief was immediate. Her heart and then her form returned to Earth-tone red. After hugging Daddy, she broke free to explore.

"If you ever need anything, just call me," Daddy Double HimACane said, his voice roaring into her My Ears before rising wind speed snatched it away. "No winds are more powerful than mine!"

Before Cloud could stray, Mother Cloud stepped forward and grabbed her arm. Cloud stiffened, shivered, and recoiled. Then she moved obediently toward Mother, who touched her own forehead to melt some cleansing frost. Restraining Cloud, she dabbed at the droppings that still clung to her. She moistened Cloud's feathered wisps that pointed upward, forcing them down.

"There! Your My Ears are covered. They stick out like mine," Mother Cloud said, grimacing.

Cloud turned red, dropping lower in the sky.

Mother Cloud looked down on her and continued, "Look at Daddy Double HimACane as he takes off into the air. Isn't he magnificent with his two storms of tightly packed winds and Resources? When I met him he just had one, but now he's even more impressive! He takes over so I can relax and know I'm protected." Mother smiled and lifted her head high.

She leaned close to Cloud and whispered, "Now, as young as you are, you need preparation to one day attract and keep your own powerful Protect Her." She reached into Cloud's inner layer and attached a hook.

"Keep your cirrus layers feathered over it at all times to avoid over Expose Her. It might scare your future Double HimACane away!"

Cloud jumped. She turned her blurry focus toward Mother Cloud. For the first time she noticed that Mother Cloud might have *one* My Sight, but even that one was well hidden and closed. She scanned the area all around Mother for Feed Her Bands like Daddy's that could provide nourishment. There were none. She moved closer to Mother, seeking direct warmth. Instead she met a chilly breeze. Shaking, she floated further away from Mother Cloud. The whole world seemed colder and smaller somehow.

Following a trail of welcomed, golden heat, Cloud found Daddy. When she was near him, the world seemed warmer and larger. She expanded, edged closer, and wriggled with excitement. Tilting her head up to him, she beseeched in her littlest Cloud voice, "Daddy, show me how to catch a bird!"

"That's my Special Cloud! Turn your little face up to the sunshine. To see your smile, I'd rampage throughout all the skies, land, and sea!" he promised. "We'll find your bird together."

"Goodie!" She raised her misty cloud trail to step onto one of his dimensional Feed Her Bands. Each one nourished her and raised her higher. She molded herself to his back. A quiet tremble and low hum from within him excited her senses. Controlled power gave way to a whirling display of wind, thunder, and ferocious speed. They shot away.

Mother Cloud found herself alone, buffeted by tailwinds. She shrank, and her center darkened. She shook herself free of residual debris and arranged colored bits and pieces into her stratum. She pulled a nearby Reflect Her Cloud over and preened. The golden cast reappeared; her form expanded. She floated away in regal grandeur, greeting random, littler clouds.

Daddy Double HimACane squealed to a stop. "My Cloud, there's a seagull for you up ahead. What do you like about these birds, little one?"

"Daddy, they can fly anywhere! Their wings are beautiful and white. They can soar on the wind and fly right through the clouds. And they're not afraid of being alone. They're strong and brave and pretty!"

"Then you shall have one of your own! Step off and stay beside me."

Daddy leaned over. He encircled a gull of purest white with his band of gale-force winds. Cloud flushed with excitement. The trapped bird briefly escaped, one broken wing folded up. Desperate to fly, it pounded the air with its single wing. When Daddy Double HimACane's winds moved in to surround it completely, the bird hurled itself against each side of its unexpected prison over and over. Finally it sank onto its back and lay very still. Its dislodged feathers blew in disarray around its lifeless body.

Cloud's heart quickly drained into white. For a moment she turned away. Daddy expanded, raised his head high, and offered her the seagull.

"No, Daddy," she responded in a different voice, "I've changed my mind."

Daddy Double HimACane paused and stared at her uncertainly. The lifeless bird fell through his opened hands. It fell down, down, down through the clouds, through the open sky, to the Earth below. Daddy took a deep breath and re-strengthened himself.

"Forget the bird, then. How about flying with me high and low, from Earth to sky and back again?" he suggested, winds swirling. Lightning sparked from his back. Thunder bullets ricocheted through the sky. Cloud climbed on.

"Hold on! Now we're going down!" Daddy's words echoed into her My Ears.

The extreme gravitational change brought Cloud's tummy almost up into her throat. Winds snatched joyous gasps from her mouth. With renewed vitality, he whirled upward at mind-numbing speed. Cloud screamed with glee as his wind actions fed and produced a smaller funnel of her very own. They reversed course. In a few moments green and brown Earth obstacles loomed into view. Just as it seemed they would crash headlong into a mountain, Daddy switched course once again. Right before dropping fully into the white-capped ocean waters below, Daddy ripped off his outer coverings and directed her to do the same. Cloud obeyed, removing the layers that clothed her. She was unable to see well and suddenly felt very, very warm, then very, very cold. Daddy didn't touch her but she knew he was oh-so-near in the dark waters. She held her breath.

On the way up and out she pulled her coverings back on quickly, avoiding Daddy's My Sight. An alarm went off inside her. She found herself wearing new Trapped My Sight glasses. To accommodate this uncomfortable scenery, she pulled them off and replaced them with deeper My Rose-Colored glasses, an emergency defense she received earlier from Mother and Daddy. At that exact moment an unusual fog rolled in from under a nearby bridge.

Cloud told herself this encounter with Daddy meant that she was special, Number One! She didn't need her hook with him, not at all. Then she felt a smile break through her darkened layers. Daddy Double HimACane, with his Cloud attachment, rose higher. She felt like a bird! Laughing together, they traveled the skies.

On the way home, Daddy Double HimACane suggested that Cloud hop off and wait while he attended to some "Daddy things." After a while she floated closer to see Daddy, tipping her head up. His gigantic mass hovered under a strange-looking cloud. Its top was shaped like an anvil. Its core was a sweet rosy pink that seemed hauntingly familiar to Cloud. She smiled in remembrance of Bliss Full feedings from something or someone long ago.

She watched as Daddy raised his back until his winds touched the ominous cloud's underbelly. At the point of contact, foul-smelling rains broke loose. They drenched Daddy in a short, heavy shower. His Earth My Sights grew larger and then narrowed to pinpoints. His taut, rigid winds loosened ever so slightly. Cloud gasped and covered her mouth as a pale, pink glow emanated from her middle. His body spasmed in whooshing hiccups. He lost altitude so fast he almost fell below Cloud's place in the sky.

"Daddy, can we go now? And what's the name of that funny cloud?" she asked. "It smells icky! And now you do too," she added in a whisper.

Daddy looked at her quickly and then looked away. "It's a Toxic Rain Cloud, Special Her. It's not good for Clouds like you. Daddies relax that way, little one. It's fine for us to do, but only after sunset."

Cloud slipped on some Clear View My Sight glasses and shuddered when Daddy Double HimACane looked at her. Both of his My Sights were obscured, dazed with a cloud cover she'd never seen before. She opened her mouth to speak but held her breath instead.

"Climb onto my back. Let's fly around a bit on the way home." Daddy smiled a strange smile.

Cloud didn't smile on the flight home. Daddy Double HimACane didn't act like he was playing. He careened one way and then the other. She felt the contraction of My Will Power that Daddy summoned to avoid flying too low too fast. He narrowly missed smacking into another Double HimACane, who wheeled around to chase them.

"What do you think you're doing? You could've destroyed us both!" the other Double HimACane yelled.

"Don't start with me! I couldn't see well! Something blew into one of My Sights!" Daddy shot back.

The two forces faced each other. For a moment Cloud thought Daddy Double HimACane was going to whirl into him on purpose. The other Double HimACane, twin funnels pulsing red, glowered at Daddy. At last he veered away.

When they reached Mother Cloud's space near Earth, her back was turned to them. Next to her were the garment layers and cloud knickknacks she collected every day. Daddy quickly removed Cloud from his back. He didn't even turn around to make sure she was all right as he usually did. Instead he swooped down on Mother Cloud. Clutching her in his whirlwinds, he twisted her around, whooping and bellowing. She laughed and surrendered to the dance. A pink gleam shone through Mother Cloud. She giggled and lowered her head. When Daddy Double HimACane slowed the pace, she raised her head and paused, sniffing the air around him.

"Have you been soaking up Toxic Rain again?" she demanded, backing away from him.

"Trust you to ruin a good mood!" His breezes compressed, releasing strong gales. His clouds darkened to blue-black. Thunder rumbled from within him. Lightning bolted from his face in jagged zigzags. Cloud froze in place. "I work for hours every day, circulating and churning better than any Single or Double HimACane I know! I tear through land and sea! I've found the key to success! My twin winds un-Earth more than enough twin Resource streams to provide us with all a Cloud family would ever need or want. All you have to do is collect them. And what do you do with them? Store them? No! You trade them for frivolous nothings—all day, every day. You refuse to learn how to travel on your own. You cling to your friends or to me for rides, just like you're a Little Cloud!"

"You told me to let it be you! You wanted to be the one to fly me everywhere! You *told* me to cling to you!" Mother Cloud's face turned black. Raindrops released and clung. They froze, refusing to fall. She sucked them up, belly bulging lower and turning gray. "And I decorate the Debris Resources with bows so they look pretty for our family. I thought you noticed that!"

Daddy roared up and blew away. Cloud followed him in jerks. The warm light oozed out of her, leaving emptiness that ached in her middle. She trailed uncertainly along the path of sheared clouds Daddy left in his wake. Then she gasped and covered her mouth at a horrible sight. Daddy was pressing up to another Toxic Rain Cloud.

Cloud flounced back over to Mother Cloud.

"Why couldn't you just be nice to Daddy?" she demanded. "You make him soak up more Toxic Rain. I hate you!"

"Don't talk to me like that, Cloud! I'll tell your Father!" threatened Mother Cloud.

In a little while Daddy Double HimACane flew down to Cloud and whirled in front of her face. His face was crimson and his My Sights looked yellow and mean.

"Never speak to your mother with disrespect! Do you hear me?"

Cloud nodded. Her head hurt. Her wispy clouds floated about in opposing directions. Her My Sights crossed and then faded out.

But the next morning everything seemed normal again. Cloud moved slowly toward her parents and noticed a huge Elephant in the Living Room that Mother and Daddy either didn't see or wouldn't acknowledge.

"How's my beautiful Cloud this fine morning?" Daddy asked. "Today we'll plow across the Earth and see what we can scatter around. Mother Cloud, you don't want to come with us, do you?" he asked while focusing only on Cloud.

"Oh no." Mother shook her head. "I'll be making a visit to Wind Shear Beauty. Some of my cirrus wisps need care." She noticed Daddy's lack of attention, dropping lower and becoming smaller. She used a smaller voice too and fluffed up her cirrus layers.

"But I do need a ride—shall I call my Cloud friend, the one who's forced to drive herself around without a powerful Him like you, or will you take me yourself? My friend may have other things to do…"

Daddy didn't hear her. He and Cloud had already left.

As the sun faded, Daddy was again at Mother Cloud's side. She chatted away, newly coiffed edges stiffly in place. Daddy paid less and less attention to her as he absorbed more and more Toxic Rain.

In the days that followed Cloud saw less and less of Mother. Daddy whirled around more than ever. He took Mother to Weather Support Space. She didn't return. Cloud spent much more time with Daddy and with Mother's one or two Cloud friends. They played with her. She even spent the night with them more than once. That seemed strange. Cloud missed Daddy. She contracted from the other Cloud mothers and clung to Daddy even harder when he returned for her.

Eventually Mother came home—many months later. She was smaller and colder than before and hardly moved around at all. Daddy seemed to hover around her more now.

Cloud was left alone. As darkness closed in, her center turned gray and she burrowed down into her nighttime nest. Visions of Daddy disappearing someday crowded in on her. As she surrendered to the thoughts, they became very real.

"Daddy seems to be fading. He's becoming almost trans-parent, thinning out and obliterating. His My Sights are combining into one and changing into something else. Oh no! He's gone! I'll never see him again," she sobbed. The scenario repeated itself over and over until sleep overtook her.

The next morning Cloud was ill. Nourishment rejected itself, and her center was empty and aching. Her outer layers radiated an unnatural flush. Moisture beads trickled from her head. Mother Cloud floated above her and then called for Daddy.

He rushed to Cloud's side, declaring, "I wish I could take your pain away and make it mine." He sprinkled her with warm rain and massaged her back and arms. "We'll have some new adventures soon, Little Cloud. Remember I'm always here for you."

As she cuddled up to him and fell asleep, she smiled through her discomfort, secure that she was still Number One.

Chapter 3
Hope Full and Hope Fall

Cloud powers herself up to a Storm, winning Daddy's approval. Mother Cloud voices disapproval and instructs her on female disempowerment. Cloud experiences a secret event with Daddy that creates mixed messages in her heart. She returns to Mother for further discussion on powerlessness and attraction. Then she returns to Daddy, who suddenly supports Mother's opinion.

A s Cloud grew older her round and fluffy form narrowed in the middle and widened on the top and bottom. One day she unfurled her curvy legs and Daddy Double HimACane halted abruptly. He blew over to Cloud, his winds whirling a special whistle. "Your form is quite something!" he announced.

Mother Cloud smiled into outer space, chewing on more and more sugarcane. "Yes, she's shaped just like me."

Daddy's twin My Sights glared silently at Mother Cloud, whose legs were almost identical to Cloud's, but whose middle girth had increased to more than twice its former size.

Energized by Daddy's reassuring warmth behind her, Cloud tipped herself onto her back and glowed. In sheer delight, she opened her mouth and blew laughter up into the heavens. Daddy waved at Mother as he took Cloud down to the sea again. Mother Cloud covered her mouth with her hand, grabbed some nearby sugarcane, and turned away.

When Daddy and Cloud approached the water, Daddy waited for her to remove her outer coverings as he removed his own. He didn't look at her. She didn't look at him. She raised her head, expanding, then dropped her head, contracting and reddening. Her winds circled in opposing directions and picked up greater speed than in the past. Small lightning bolts sparked from her in different directions. Daddy Double HimACane didn't appear to notice. Cloud smiled all the way home, My Rose-Colored glasses neatly in place.

Soon Him Clouds appeared on the horizon. Some made silly remarks and fell all over themselves to get Cloud's attention. She laughed, but she wasn't interested in Him Clouds. At times she was dreamily romantic, lost in thoughts of unknown Double HimACanes. Rosy, thicker cumulus layers sprang out from her form. Soft winds ruffled around and through her cirrus tendrils in a melodic hum. At other times she exploded for no particular reason into fits of misery and fury. The new layers darkened. Winds intensified, erupting into small, angry squalls. Electrical currents fizzled up, delivering a small shock to anyone nearby. Heavy rains pounded down. Then all was quiet again. Her substantial new layers remained. She had surpassed Mother Cloud altogether!

"I think it's time to change your name to Storm Cloud, Storm for short," Daddy Double HimACane said after observing one of Cloud's latest gusty displays.

Mother Cloud's face tinted to deep green. Then she blanched. "Storm?" She trembled. "With all that lightning? Why, the next thing you know, you'll be upgrading her to…to…" She shook her head, deflating and sinking a level lower toward the ground.

Storm, acknowledging her new name, lifted her head, puffed up, and smiled at Daddy. Her added cloud volume swelled and shone. She moved around easily with the energy of newfound wind speed. Buoyed higher in the sky than before, she leaned up on misty tiptoes to kiss his blustery cheek. She wrapped her arms around his powerful neck. He rubbed her shoulders and legs and back. This time he also rubbed her neck and the tops of her arms. Storm's winds reversed and hummed along with this new attention. She glanced downward to Mother Cloud, who looked at them both, averted her face, and floated away.

Daddy Double HimACane shrugged, surveyed Storm once again, and nodded. "Your Mother has many fears," he said, rotating away.

Storm listened intently. In the distance she heard the unmistakable trickle of Toxic Rain, a familiar sound when Daddy was near.

Later, Mother Cloud called up to Storm. "Come down here, please. Stay in this airspace with me. I've traded Debris Resources for some lovely outer garments to add sheen to your new form. I have to admit you've become quite a storm. You make a pretty display. Just make sure you Stay a Storm. Enough is enough!"

"But why, Mother Cloud?" Storm wanted to know. "Storms are much more powerful than Clouds. Clouds just kind of sit there. They're air masses with never-changing temperature and humidity. They try to look interesting by wearing different-colored coverings like the ones you're wrapping me up in now. Someday I'd like to be even bigger than a Storm—maybe even a whirling energy of some kind."

Mother Cloud turned away. Storm impatiently shook loose the garment Mother Cloud had arranged on her.

"The problem is…" Mother glanced around nervously, lowering her head and her voice. "If a Storm's clouds become very dense, they can produce funnel clouds leading to tornadoes. If they gather enough moisture, if winds and weather conditions are just right, then over time…there's a chance—only a chance, mind you—that…that…"

"That what, Mother Cloud? Come out with it!" demanded Storm.

"That they…that you…might become…a…a…HerACane!" Mother Cloud whispered violently. She stared straight at Storm and covered her face with her hands, shaking uncontrollably.

"I knew it, I knew it!" yelped Storm in excitement. "I just knew it was possible…that someday one Earth My Sight could show…or maybe I could even have two—*Double* My Sight—just like Daddy's!" She fairly danced around Mother's trembling form. Somersaulting in joy, she created little, cyclonic winds. They swirled about her like a layered miniskirt.

"Enough!" ordered Mother Cloud sharply. Storm stopped at once. Mother's voice had a tone Storm had never heard before. "This is no laughing matter! Your My Sight is showing right now—cover it up!"

"Mother Cloud, what's wrong with having a My Sight that shows? Why don't you have even one? How can you see? Daddy has two! Why can't I have just one?"

"Storm, get this straight: First, you need to cover your Earth My Sight like I do to show yourself as young and appealing and to attract someone to take care of you. Second, yes, Daddy Double HimACane has Double My Sight. The greater the power of the winds, the smaller the My Sights become. If My Will Power decreases, the winds decrease.

Without careful monitoring My Sights may enlarge and give way to EYE Space."

Mother Cloud continued. "EYE Space is nothing to fear by itself. The EYE Space of a HimACane or a HerACane is silent and weak. It's a place of total calm—no wind movement at all. It's so peaceful and still, in fact, that not even a cloud can exist for long inside of a well-developed EYE Space. So do you see? The danger is this: EYE M could indeed come right on through that EYE Space. EYE Will and EYE Will Power would arrive and overcome all else! My Sight would exit. The end would be very near. Obliteration would follow." Her voice shook.

"Luckily, EYE M, EYE Will, and EYE Will Power can be overcome. Me, My Will, and My Will Power accomplish that, and quite nicely!"

Mother Cloud cleared her throat. "Of course, this is mainly an issue for Daddy. A Double HimACane's fierce, whirling winds can churn up the land and sea around his Double My Sights. All HimACanes are masculine and forceful. Speed and fearlessness are their dominion. They're here to take care of us.

"Now a HerACane, on the other hand, is destructive. With access to so much speed from Earth My Sight, a HerACane like you might set off in the wrong direction. You could get lost…maybe forever. You might lose control and crash into something on Earth. Worse yet, no HimACane would ever want you. HimACanes don't find all that potency in a Her Cloud either feminine or attractive. As you grow older, you'll be left all alone if you don't have a HimACane. With no one to take care of you, you'd eventually obliterate. I know what I'm talking about. After all, you have a Double HimACane as a daddy because of me."

Mother Cloud smoothed her cirrus waves while looking in a Reflect Her Cloud, then continued. "They're quite a rare find. I'm very lucky. Daddy Double HimACane takes very good care of us."

She paused, her lips curving upward. She suddenly looked quite beautiful. She pointed to Daddy in the distance. "But it was all much more than luck. I can show you how to be more special than all the others. You'll be the most attractive Storm around if you'll hear my advice and apply it. When you finally have your own Double HimACane and settle down, giving birth to your own Little Clouds, you'll be safe. Being safe is far more important than the risk of allowing an EYE Space!" She smiled with tight lips, lifted her chin, and raised her head as high as she could.

Storm grew pale. She observed Mother Cloud and noticed that her light was lodged behind Daddy's, never able to shine in its own Earth Space. Storm's clouds retracted into a smaller, quieter mass.

"But Mother, even if I keep My Sight covered, I feel an EYE Space underneath—a large one—and sometimes it shows, especially when I pick up speed and the wind opens up my layers. And when I look through that open EYE Space, I become nice and still inside and out. I can see better than ever then. Things look…well…different. It makes me want to see even more."

Mother leaned in to smooth Storm's cirrus feathers firmly backward with one hand. She gazed at a My Sight and then through it into a large, sparkling EYE Space. Unable to repress a shudder, she looked away, gathered some kind of power, and swiveled back, pulling Storm's feathers down again with intensity. Storm winced.

"It's all right," Mother stated with conviction. "It's only a small EYE Space—a break in the clouds and nothing more. Keep it hidden; use My Sight instead to help you appear…well, non-threatening. And cover that too! Don't dwell on this. Over time it should repair itself. Here's some sugarcane to relieve any pain. And remember to cover your Earth Ears! As I said before, they stick out, just like mine used to. Not a pretty sight. Whatever you need to hear, you'll hear from Daddy Double HimACane and me. And whatever you need to see, you'll see through Daddy's My

Sight and even mine, too. If you must, then use My Rose-Colored glasses for a better view. Leave it at that!"

Mother's layers billowed out. Wind threatened to stir.

Storm sighed. Her innermost winds receded. "All right, Mother Cloud. I understand. Just show me what to do. My new name will be Stay a Storm, Storm for short. And I'll change my shape to attract and hang onto a Him, maybe even a Double Him, like this. Is this right? With that, Storm twisted herself into a sleek form and attached the hook at the edge. She was careful to arrange her feathered layers over its sharp end to hide the hidden Commit Meant hook.

Mother Cloud sighed in relief. "Keep that little surprise well covered or the Hims will all move away! For now, Storm, we must find you a sweet Him Cloud to practice with."

"*We* must?" Storm whirled around toward Mother Cloud, her cirrus feathers stiffening up.

"Oh, I meant you must, of course." Mother Cloud gave a frosty smile into a nearby Reflect Her Cloud and moved away, her head held high.

Storm floated down near Earth the next day. She sighed while watching Daddy Double HimACane romp, race, and plunder through fields and cities. She finally grabbed his attention by floating right in front of his space.

"Daddy Double HimACane, tell me the difference between My Sight and EYE Sight."

He paused, his tornadoes laying bare the forest he was pillaging. "Storm, this must be important for you to interrupt me like this. All right. HimACanes or HerACanes are created by My Will and My Will Power—and when more of that is added, intense winds develop. *Increased* My Will Power keeps the energy revolving. *More* My Will Power holds this new vision together. Even *more* than that…well, who knows. There's always room for more!"

Daddy took a huge breath. He sucked up a Dust Devil Tube, then slowly blew it out—left, right, up, and down—toward the Earth as he exhaled. Storm inhaled a bit of it too, coughed, and inhaled it more deeply. Daddy pretended not to notice.

"Don't you miss having EYE Spaces that help you see well and feel peaceful?" Storm asked.

His color darkened. "There was a time when events in my life were painful. As a result, my hard-earned My Sight weakened, so much so that EYE Space appeared from beneath. EYE Space deepened. My winds slowed and spread out and my storms weakened. Complete breakdown was near. My life was in peril. But through intense struggle and use of My Will Power, my wind forces increased. They actually created a Double! But the danger was very real. Let this be a warning to you. Fast action saves lives. If you stay there long enough EYE Space opens up into…EYE Sight! It's lethal to linger there. EYE M awaits!"

Daddy whirled and shook as he spoke. Then he turned his My Sights directly toward her. "You're quite beautiful and very special, Storm. Let your mother be your guide. Now, don't get me wrong here. I sometimes find *myself* looking up through EYE Space. I become amazingly relaxed, and on occasion I stay there long enough to catch a glimpse of EYE M. Oh yes, I salute as I whirl by! But I don't want to get caught up in that area, not until I'm ready and willing to …well…give up and dissolve completely. "So," he summarized, "you and I can have fun watching powerful weather together, but please just Stay a Storm. Find a special HimACane to take care of you. That's your mission."

Storm floated off to think about all she had learned. As she crossed certain points near Earth, she heard faint music with whispered, special words. Would she be special enough to find a special HimACane, maybe even a Double HimACane, someday? She hovered near the music and then sadly traveled further.

There's hope, thought Storm. I have to become more special than all other Her Clouds, or Her Storms, or even Stay a Storms. I'll attract a HimACane, maybe even a Double one! I'll be whatever he wants me to be. That's all there is to it.

As Mother Cloud had promised, their sky space soon teemed with other clouds and storms, sometimes from morning until night. They were allowed inside the protective confines of Storm's family airspace "to make sure that Storm doesn't step outside our world to find entertainment on her own," whispered Mother Cloud to Daddy.

Each of Cloud's "friends" floated or blew home after a long night of music and games. One at a time they called out, "goodnight to Cloud Family Country Club!" Storm wondered if the friends really liked her or only liked the fun. Her winds blew one way and then the other. She increased in size and then became small and red. It would be so nice to visit others' cloud spaces too one day, she thought briefly. Mother Cloud and Daddy always seemed to have a reason why that couldn't happen. She couldn't fight them, especially not Daddy. So she sighed and smiled instead, allowing her form to blow one way and then the other. She wondered if she was creating a double life of some kind.

"Remember our first tiny little house?" Mother Cloud said, nudging Daddy. "Things have certainly changed, with all your Debris Resources for us. Now, look around our special upgraded neighborhood and just imagine what might happen if Storm left our home to travel about on her own!"

Daddy nodded gravely. He smiled and shook his head, thinking back to their modest beginnings. He lifted his head high, puffed himself up, and looked around. Then he frowned at the danger just barely in sight near the bottom of his vision.

Mother Cloud showed Storm how to adorn herself and accentuate her best features. "Your My Sight underneath is huge, just like Daddy Double HimACane's! We certainly need to minimize that message.

Hims will suspect that you can see for yourself. What a turnoff! To focus only on how you look, we'll add some dark color here and feather your wisps to cover My Sight. Your extremities are splendid, just like mine. Show them off with short garment layers. Move slowly—you tend to fly around like a bird! Not the right message."

Storm became smaller. She floated away to consult a Reflect Her Cloud. Her cloud layers slumped forward, then receded. Mother Cloud met her there. She stared hard at Storm's center.

"Hold your middle in! And stand up straight!"

Storm looked at her modest form and then at Mother Cloud's voluminous center. Her head hurt. She suddenly energized into a Tropical Disturbed Dance, her winds picking up speed and circling around in opposite directions. She sucked in her middle. She sucked up the chaos inside and stayed Storm as she was told. From then on, she gazed into every Reflect Her Cloud that passed by. Her form shimmered with colorful costumes. She arranged flower petals into bright confetti along with streamers and twigs that perched among her face feathers. She glittered when the sun's rays were upon her. On closer inspection, however, emptiness inside marred the gilded image. Her heart center was turning gray. An Ice Train began to form.

Chapter 4

Power Full And Power Fall

Storm struggles to learn freedom of movement. She changes form from sizable Storm back down to Cloud as Mommy and Daddy disempower her once again by removing her Firebird. She powers back up when she finds a smaller Him Cloud boyfriend. She experiences intimate oneness with him amid mixed messages from Mother Cloud. She tries to support Him Cloud during his family crisis, gets introduced to Toxic Rain, and falls into a new kind of love. Storm tries to grow up by leaving home and attending a certain school, but she gives up a year later after she learns that numbers classes will be the next agenda. She returns home to Mother and Daddy.

During a weather school gathering, Storm climbed an observation tower to scan the sky. She noticed a handsome Him Cloud. He drew an admiring crowd of Her Clouds and even some Her Storms. Storm joined the throng of Hers and giggled. Unable to capture his attention, she unfurled her hook. She carefully shrouded it in a thin veil of misty vapors and approached the gathering group. In a show of hushed drama, she lowered her head slightly, then tilted and raised it.

"Listen," she intoned. "I'll tell you all a secret. That Him Cloud has done it before. He'll do it again—so get ready for A BROKEN HEART!"

Her performance worked! All the Her Clouds within earshot scattered.

The lonely Him Cloud turned to Storm. Retracting her hook, she wondered what to do with him now that she had caught him. He shone a pastel light that permeated her empty heart. It disappeared quickly, leaving her empty once again. It was lighter than Perfect Love or Mother and Daddy's, but it felt much the same. Storm had more My Will Power than he did, which was nice for a change. *She* pulled *him* along. *She* was the one who decided where they moved or if they moved at all.

Soon the two of them became a pair among the daily and nightly group of noisy, festive clouds and storms. Him Cloud gazed up at Storm with admiration and affection. Mother Cloud nodded at Storm. She welcomed the Him Cloud into activities meant just for the family. Him Cloud gazed up at Daddy Double HimACane with admiration and affection too. Daddy smiled down at Him Cloud, reminding him that Storm was special. Him Cloud nodded solemnly in agreement. Mother smiled and moved Daddy away with her by chatting and pointing to Toxic Rain Clouds to hook his attention.

Storm and Him Cloud celebrated their newfound couple's freedom by inhaling from Dust Devil Tubes just like Mother and Daddy did, but only when they weren't watching.

The time came when Storm was deemed old enough to travel around the sky without clinging to Him Cloud or Daddy Double HimACane's back. Mother shuddered, but Daddy expanded, raised his head, and presented Storm with her own golden Firebird. She billowed out and up into greater dimensions, her pink deepening and golden edges unfurling. Smiling, she directed the Firebird's movements toward her desired destinations. She rode atop its back, guiding its wings with enthusiasm.

During her first attempts, she almost knocked into the sides of one or two other clouds. She over corrected herself, increasing her speed and smiling at her own My Will Power. Winds blew over her top cirrus layers, exposing a break in her clouds. A deeply imbedded My Sight flashed in the sun. She glanced back at Mother Cloud for encouragement. Mother Cloud covered her mouth and turned away. Very soon Storm overheard Mother Cloud whispering to Daddy Double HimACane.

Daddy stopped smiling. He blew over to Storm. "All right, there's a new plan. Let's let Him Cloud keep the Firebird. He can be the Drive Her and pick you up every day. You can hold onto his tailwinds. It will help him feel important," Daddy explained.

Storm turned white, then crimson. Her expansive clouds and winds receded into one small, compact air mass. Her center darkened and her head dropped. She released her wind speed and thinned out, dark cirrus clouds tinged in red. She removed herself from the Firebird and from then on became Him Powered. Her name changed back from Storm to Cloud. She surrendered, hanging on to Him Cloud's tailwinds while he directed the Firebird. Cloud closed her My Sight tightly and made sure her cirrus waves were properly arranged. Mother Cloud passed by and tossed them a deep green Cloud Cover. Later, Cloud snuggled up to Him Cloud.

Mother turned her head, smiled, and left to search for Daddy's company. He was usually busy with his friends: Dust Devil Tubes, Toxic Rain, and his special form of entertainment, Boxed Music.

Him Cloud and Cloud invited Daddy over to their space and played a sample of their music in front of him. Cloud upgraded herself a bit, gyrating to the beat and looking at Daddy for approval. Daddy Double HimACane frowned. He told them there were two kinds of music— Boxed Music and "just plain noise!"

When they played their own music from then on, it was behind a Cloud Cover. Cloud turned the music down low, contracted, and felt her winds blow in opposite directions around her face. Daddy passed by, listened, and shook his head. He blew dust from Dust Devil Tubes as he flew off at sunset in search of Toxic Rain.

Cloud really didn't notice Daddy now. She wrapped herself in the arms of Him Cloud. They spent all their time together. Daddy and Mother Cloud stayed far enough away to allow them long evenings of privacy. Cloud's head hurt as her affection for Him Cloud grew during these times. Daddy reminded her that she must always stay purest white. Mother looked away and offered the pair another blanket while praising Cloud for her purity in all conditions. Opposing winds circled around her, gaining strength.

Her name returned to Storm. The two cuddled more. They cuddled longer. New, pulsing music drifted up from between them. It was impossible for her to resist anymore. Eventually she became one with Him Cloud. When she looked in a Reflect Her Cloud, her inner white areas seemed dark now. She assured herself that Commit Meant would come later. She also reassured herself that she even wanted that from Him. But deep within her center, a gray shadow deepened and spread.

Over time, Him Cloud felt safe enough to confide in Storm. "My Daddy Cloud and Mother Cloud won't be together anymore," he said sadly. "Daddy's leaving. After all these years he wants a new Her Cloud. Tonight is the last night my Cloud family will all be together. Will you float over with me to spend some goodbye time with them?" His face turned pale. His belly hung low and dark with the weight of unshed rain.

Storm waited. Him Cloud waited. A raindrop tear escaped and ran down his side. Her insides quivered. From somewhere deep within, purple colors flushed into her heart, energizing her. She expanded and gasped, lifting higher. She took a deep breath and nodded. "I want to be there for you," was all she managed.

Storm and Him Cloud mingled with his mother, brother, and sister Clouds. When the Daddy Cloud joined them, Storm averted her face. She tried to radiate sunlight from behind her as rain begged for release inside her belly. Her head hurt. Winds circulated in opposing directions.

This strange Last Supper began. Each of Him Cloud's family members, directed in silence by the Daddy Him Cloud, ceremoniously approached a huge Toxic Rain Cloud that looked a lot like the ones Daddy loved. Storm obediently floated up to bump under the cloud too. A brief, gentle drizzle doused her form. She sniffed a familiar, strong odor. The shower felt cool and refreshing.

In a few minutes Storm felt burning, luscious warmth spread throughout her entire length. She felt her clouds expand into luxurious crests of loving rose and Courage Us purple, highlighted with unabashed gold. This was even better than the first purple flush she had felt! She gazed at Him Cloud's whole family. They had changed! They seemed to smile at one another in love and understanding. The air space around them glittered softly with bliss and peace. She floated nearer to the illusion. She saw it all so clearly.

"I know I have an EYE Space now! It even feels like love—like a Commit Meant!" she rejoiced to herself. "Maybe someday I'll even find EYE M in that space. Perfect Vision!"

The rest of the evening passed in a haze of comfort, peace, and joy. Despite the intense peace, she picked up speed and her energy upgraded, a strange turn of events.

On the way home Storm barely noticed Him Cloud. "No wonder Daddy Double HimACane loves Toxic Rain!" she thought.

The next morning she rushed to poke her face into a Reflect Her Cloud. She saw Her My Sight but no EYE Space. "I'll find it again—and soon!" she promised herself.

Storm and Him Cloud drifted close to a large crowd of assorted weather formations. The strong stench of Toxic Rain permeated the air. Dozens of clouds and storms laughed and danced about. Several clouds formed a pipeline that directed raucous music from Earth to the surrounding skies. The noise drowned out all conversation. Him Cloud grabbed Storm and dragged her into the crowd. "Let's dance!"

She contracted into a small cloud, too inhibited to respond to the beat. As much as she wanted to fade into the background, she knew it would be dangerous to "sit it out." Another Her Storm or Her Cloud could easily float over. Him Cloud might leave her for a more special Her. She would be alone. She shivered.

"I'll be right back," murmured Storm. She spiraled upward toward a particularly dark Toxic Rain Cloud. Bumping under it, she sighed in relief. Heavy rain pounded down. She soaked up every last drop before moving on to a smaller one, then another. Saturated with all the Toxic Rain her layers could hold, she returned to Him Cloud. She held her head up high. Her body swayed in confident rhythm to the deafening music. Guitars screeched. Drums crashed.

"All right! Let's dance!" Storm whirled the bemused Him Cloud around, laughing. She twirled and danced faster and faster. She laughed as the sky and the moon and the stars danced, too. Suddenly they spun around in frightening chaos—then silence, as she fell into a blackout.

When she knew her surroundings once again, Storm found herself next to Him Cloud. Together they faced Daddy Double HimACane. His winds increased to twin gales at the sight of her distress.

Storm couldn't speak. Her clouds contracted into a sickly gray. Her winds howled. Rain burst forth in torrents. Him Cloud explained to Daddy that Toxic Rain was responsible for her condition. Mother Cloud peered anxiously from behind Daddy's hulking form. She scurried away to deal with Storm's garments. Daddy's winds diminished. He pulled Storm into one of his My Sights as Him Cloud sailed away. Storm's inner layer heaved. She retched again and again. Toxic Rain exploded from within her.

Daddy Double HimACane held her close. "It's all right, Storm. You just need to learn how much Toxic Rain is enough." He smiled. "This can happen at first. You're Tox Sick. It takes practice."

The next day Storm noticed the Elephant in the Living Room again. Nobody, of course, mentioned it. She carefully avoided it altogether. When Storm saw him again, Him Cloud acted like nothing unusual had happened. Their friends laughed at her, though, describing her party antics, of which she remembered nothing. She pretended to laugh too. The Elephant appeared and laughed as well, trumpeting loudly. He was becoming more familiar all the time.

She was a smaller storm now. Her layers tightened and shrank into a more controlled image of her former self. Deep inside, the gray shadow in her center darkened and trembled. "I miss being a Little Cloud. Everything looked pretty then. I hate My Sight more than I hate being sick or laughed at," she told herself. "I'll wait a bit before searching for my EYE Space again. I'll figure out what I did wrong with the Toxic Rain and do it right next time. But no matter what, I need it to find that EYE Space!"

After several months Storm tried again. She and Him Cloud met with friends. Storm traveled toward a smaller, lighter Toxic Rain Cloud.

After bathing in it, she thought her EYE Space appeared. Quickly it was gone. She aimed for and found another Toxic Rain Cloud. Its rains served only to deepen her darkness. Her winds and storms increased in volume. Thunder rumbled from within her. Zaps of lightning scattered nearby clouds. They narrowly missed Him Cloud, who reversed his course. Cautiously, he accompanied her from a distance. Again, her rains poured down, increasing into flash floods. At last her winds died down.

Storm, dripping water and breathing heavily from exertion, whooshed home. She passed by Daddy Double HimACane without a word. She knew the truth. It might not seem like it, but she was making progress. She had upgraded to a tropical depression. With determination, she downgraded herself once again to Stay a Storm.

Every few months Storm struggled once more to find her elusive EYE Space. She craved that bliss, no matter what the cost. Him Cloud was usually with her. She pressed up to small, medium, and large Toxic Clouds. She approached Toxic Clouds of gray, black, and purple-black. She was never Tox Sick again, at least not in the retching kind of way. The Toxic Rain stayed down. Her EYE Space, when she did feel it, disappeared quickly.

The final result was always a thunderstorm followed by heavy surface rains that produced shallow runoff and localized flooding, but no real cleansing. Him Cloud stoically floated by her side. His movements were sluggish now. Storm was forced to look backward at him much of the time. To provide him with motivation, she gathered wind speed and pushed him from behind or used her hook on his underbelly. She even tried charging him in a full frontal assault. On occasion Storm's efforts caused his billowy white fluff to darken. Once or twice he moved forward abruptly, almost resembling a storm. Predictably, he quickly returned to his passive, unruffled Him Cloud form.

Soon it was time for Storm to make a decision. She watched as other clouds and storms transitioned, floating away from their parents for a while. Cloud Academies near and far offered preparation for various weather skills. Some encouraged quiet movement and self-preservation. Another type enhanced creative skills within quiet, mutable clouds. The results were brilliant displays of color and substance to decorate the skies. Others taught electrical interaction among storms, resulting in powerful extravaganzas of lightning, thunder, and bountiful rains. Still others, reserved for a very few, oversaw the evolution and production of the rare and potent HerACane. Those would be studied at close range and under supervision, and never released, of course!

Him Cloud planned to attend Cloud Academy near home. "Why don't you go to Storm Sanctuary near me," he suggested. "You'd be taught more about how to Stay a Storm. After that we could be mates for life."

Storm studied him. He was loyal and kind. She had spent three years getting to know him. The consistent problem was his size and speed. Even though he changed color and form periodically, he chose to remain a quiet, unassuming cloud. Storm was several times his size. She tested her spark capacity. Yes, she also had several times his voltage.

She glanced past Him Cloud. Certain things didn't seem to change. All around her was a luxurious expanse. The space she lived in was huge. Daddy Double HimACane, saturated with Toxic Rain, isolated himself now. His winds slowed precipitously and his My Sights widened. An application of My Will Power narrowed them to tiny dots once again. Tropical Disturbed Dances embedded inside of him threatened to spark without warning.

Mother Cloud was also in a world of her own making. She arranged the day's collection of Earth Debris. She fussed over cloud garments. She repeatedly calculated Daddy's intake of Toxic Rain while lecturing him and supplying him with more. During those times her voice reverberated and her cloud form approximated a storm, reddening and expanding.

She would suddenly glance around nervously, patting down her layers, and withdraw into her usual small, dark-centered cloud form.

Storm imagined her life with Him Cloud. She pictured herself in the confines of the local Storm Sanctuary. Poignant, haunting music drifted into her My Ears. Even without Courage Us, Toxic Rain inside of her, Storm drew herself up somehow. "I've decided," she told an astonished Him Cloud, Daddy Double HimACane, and Mother Cloud, "to fly off far, far away to Storm Surge Lead Her Ship Study. I need to leave soon."

"May we come too?" Daddy and Him Cloud asked.

Mother leaned forward and whispered, "Why would you want to *do* that to yourself? I have some Romantic HimACane books for you to read and also books of others' lives to distract yourself. They're in my folds. Meet me by a Reflect Her Cloud."

"No," Cloud stated with conviction, just as she had on that fateful day when she left EYE M. "I want to do what I want to do—*all by myself*. My Will! But of course I'll need to fly there by hanging onto Daddy's tailwinds," she added in a small voice.

Reaching out with a tropical wave, Storm pelted torrential rains while leaving Him Cloud. She and Mother Cloud rode on Daddy Double HimACane's back to the faraway sky space. Storm watched many other Her Storms and Her Clouds arrive. Their forms dripped with cloud garments and Earth Debris Resources.

In a few days Daddy whirled away. At last, Mother Cloud claimed her place on his back, announcing, "It's all okay. She'll no doubt find a massive HimACane at the study space and settle down!"

Meanwhile Storm turned white. She froze in place. She was alone. Within moments a large Him Storm approached. Storm's clouds feathered out and warmed to a rosy hue. For several weeks she allowed him to spin her from place to place by holding onto his tailwinds. Soon, however, other Her Storms arrived. Many were more dimensional than she.

The Him Storm looked at the others and then told her, "You'd be *perfect* if you were 10 percent smaller!"

She turned away to hide her face from him and reddened. When she looked once again, the Him had disappeared into the female throng. Storm's center was dark and heavy. She glanced hopefully at several Him Storms who blew into view. Each steered pointedly away from her, followed by an entourage of admiring, giggling, and posing Her Clouds. Storm's layers contracted into one form. She followed some scattered Her Clouds on their journey toward Toxic Rain Clouds.

Soon the routine was solidly in place. Storm attended classes on the inner workings of storm stages during the week. She listened intently, learning many important ideas. By week's end she had developed increased Ice Train from stressed My Sight. This looked even more like Mother's frozen backdrop. When she spied herself in a Reflect Her Cloud, Storm became intent on finding her EYE Space. She made plans to attend cloud gatherings "to meet new forms," she told herself. Underneath it all, she was determined to obtain Toxic Rain. Storm wore the garments that Mother had packed and followed Her Storms who were looking for Him Storms.

The result was always the same. Storm soaked herself in Toxic Rain, tried to exude Storm Attraction, also known as S.A., danced, and searched for HimACanes in the crowd.

Seeing double, she covered one My Sight and reached out blindly with the hidden hook. But by night's end she hadn't found a Double HimACane, a HimACane, or even a Him Storm. To make matters worse, the EYE Space she searched for underneath My Sight was still missing. Then all went blank as she entered a blackout.

She found herself cuddled up in the morning with a new Him Cloud. She couldn't recall what happened or how she got there. First with delight and then with horror, she realized that he belonged to one of her cloud friends. Testing, she found that this new Him Cloud could easily be pushed around, much like the one she had left behind at home. She puffed up and roared away. Her belly opened wide to release a runoff of drenching rain. It provided no relief. The inner core of heavy gray remained. She tossed aside Mother Cloud's garments and wore dark ones instead.

Him Cloud from home came to visit her several times, but it was different from before. When Him Cloud tried to wrap himself around Storm, she stiffened inside. She diffused her clouds into such a wide, thin cirrus form that Him Cloud found himself holding onto empty air instead of her.

Storm yearned to return home and contract into a Little Cloud again, wearing all white. When she pictured Mother Cloud and Daddy Double HimACane in her mind she smiled, while a raindrop slid down her face. She told herself she'd find her EYE Space somehow when she returned home to them.

At the end of one year, Daddy Double HimACane arrived. He winked with one of his My Sights and dropped below her. He gave her the "look." She performed Play Fall and landed into his outstretched Feed Her Bands, vowing never to return to Lead Her Ship Study again. Her cramped, contracted clouds stretched out, overlapping into shades of rose. Her winds picked up speed. Lightning shot out of her dark center. Her sky space blazed and crackled with released light. She sighed in relief. Even though she hadn't located her EYE Space, she had somehow managed to Stay a Storm. Daddy was still there, and Mother Cloud looked heavier. Her center bulged and drooped with increased amounts of unshed rain. Munching sugarcane, loaded up with Dust Devil Tubes, and dragging Toxic Rain Clouds along for Daddy's enjoyment, Mother brought up the rear as usual. All was just as Storm remembered it.

She tried something new. Noticing Mother Cloud's form at the bottom of the Play Fall slide, Storm called out to her and slid down toward Mother's gray, padded center. Mother looked up, staying in place until the last minute. Just before Storm's arrival, Mother offered one hand but then moved away, shaking and calling out, "No, no! You might hurt me, Storm!"

Storm fell down, down, down through the other clouds. Just when it seemed as if she would hit the ground, something or someone caught her in a safety net of some kind. When she looked around, it turned out to be the blue butterfly. Winds stirred beneath them both and gently blew them higher. Eventually she was back with Mother. She eased off the butterfly's back.

"Oh hello, Storm, you're back. Where have you been?" asked Mother, arranging garments.

Storm opened her mouth to speak but shook her head and said nothing. She searched the sky for the butterfly. It had disappeared.

Chapter 5

Family Merge Her

Storm, no longer attracted to Him Cloud, spends so much time and travel with Daddy HimACane that Mother becomes desperate. She finds a way to manipulate the situation, and a new Him Cloud appears. Storm initially resists him and his goal, but he and Mother form a kind of team. A Merge Her ceremony is planned against her will, and even Daddy—unwilling to incur Mother's wrath—joins in. Storm downgrades to Cloud. She adds Toxic Pellets and Dust Devil Tubes to her Toxic Rain supply in order to cope.

Back in her childhood airspace, Storm drew even closer to Daddy Double HimACane than before while Mother Cloud floated behind. Wherever she went, however she moved, Daddy was all around her. Together, they played sports, found adventure, and took nourishment together. She gradually enlarged and tiered out, suggesting a major upgrade in the near future. Storm and Daddy Double HimACane soaked up Toxic Rain and had secret little talks together while Mother Cloud was busy. They decided to check out airspace far away where it was much warmer.

Daddy Double HimACane suggested flying with her alone over the ocean, a scene that Storm had always loved. Mother Cloud first reddened, then turned green beneath her cirrus waves when Daddy Double HimACane announced the trip for two. Daddy promised that after selecting and arranging their new home, he and Storm would return for Mother Cloud, who was, after all, "very busy" with garments.

A week passed. Storm and Daddy returned with new airspace pictures and combined enthusiasm. As they returned, their roar and giggles grew louder. Storm felt a surge of power beneath her and within her. She relived the special time she'd had with Daddy Double HimACane. Whenever they had visited potential new cloud spaces, he introduced Storm as his Special Her. Those they encountered seemed to think Storm was his mate. Daddy had winked at her. She had smiled from ear to ear.

Now Mother Cloud followed the two in silence on their move to a home that she, Daddy's wife, had never seen. In the background and floating after Daddy and Storm from a distance, she desperately tried a new technique. She loudly mocked their efforts and the new home. Even that failed to cause an argument or in any way separate the two.

Mother Cloud's darkening form suddenly emanated light. Retreating under a localized Cloud Cover, she attached a Storm Surge Protect Her to Storm's underbelly. Success! Storm's forward energy imploded, causing a Stationary Front that blocked further movement. Mother took her place once again at Daddy's side.

In no time at all, Storm's newly diminutive, solitary form attracted a new and decorated shooting star. It shot over and braked abruptly.

Clearly labeled as an "IMP," its spotlight heralded a star-studded cloud form, glittering with brilliant Earth Debris Resources.

"Well, how do you do?" Mother Cloud gazed up admiringly at the Him Cloud who had confidently entered their space. "I think you'll like Storm. Don't you? Sometimes we just call her Cloud," she added with a wink.

The Star-Studded Him Cloud, bright jewels and Resources accenting his form, gazed at Storm in the same way that Mother gazed at him. "My daddy is also a Double HimACane, just like yours! His winds stir up millions of material treasures. Here, Storm's mother, would you like a token from my daddy, to me, to you?" He pressed a shining stone onto Mother's outer layer.

Mother Cloud swooned. She chased them out to "explore together," sending a Cloud Cover with Storm, who glared reproachfully at her. Mother Cloud checked herself in a Reflect Her Cloud and smiled. She sucked in her middle, extended her hidden hook, and left in search of Daddy Double HimACane.

Several months later Storm approached Mother Cloud for "a talk." "I have no Storm Attraction with him, Mother Cloud. It just won't work," she announced.

Mother Cloud reddened, darkened, and held a silent vigil in the dark for three days.

"You can be the one to provide the S.A. You'll regret this forever if you pass up this opportunity," were her only words.

Storm remained unmoved, shaking and turning red herself, and also gray. She approached Daddy Double HimACane and asked him for help in explaining to Mother that she just could not go through with this Merge Her. His reply drained the color from her face.

"Sorry you feel that way, but Mother arranged special gifts from the Debris Resources I stirred up on Earth. She wants to present them during the Merge Her ceremony. I don't want problems there, so act like a good Her Cloud for now. Be an actress until after they're opened, please." Daddy Double HimACane winked, but his mouth was tight.

Storm felt a sharp, twisted pain inside her middle. Making sure she was alone, she found soothing Toxic Rain. Then she eased quietly away toward Mother Cloud's Toxic Pellet stash.

"I never use them, but just in case," Mother Cloud had explained many months ago, when introducing the hardened form of Toxic Rain. Storm now knew for sure that she was the "case" in question. She decided Mother Cloud was right. She looked to the left. On her own, she had no Resources. She looked to the right. She had found no purpose since leaving Storm Lead Her Ship Studies Academy without finishing when numbers work was required. She looked up. Her choices of Hims to take care of her had all turned out wrong. She looked down. As Mother said, this Him was her last chance. She sighed and surrendered.

Downing the Toxic Pellets, she contracted inside. She sank down low and then moved toward Star-Studded Him. Her winds quieted down. Pausing to add Toxic Rain to the mix, she downgraded to Cloud size. Her center was almost trans-parent from its drooping weight of depressed rain. Oddly enough, this time she did *not* feel her clouds expand into luxurious crests of loving rose and Courage Us purple, highlighted with unabashed gold. She and Star-Studded Him did *not* smile at one another in love and understanding. The air space around them did *not* glitter softly.

"Just call me Cloud instead of Storm," she said in the small squeaky voice she remembered from a long, long time ago. She also remembered to suck in her middle. She stood by Star-Studded Him with a smile frozen neatly into place. Delighted, Mother took pictures that she had prearranged. They were extremely Color Full. Head high, Mother took her place by Daddy. He glanced at her, then disappeared to play Boxed Music all alone.

Star-Studded Him moved forward quickly with a special Commit Meant gift for Cloud. The Merge Her performance followed. Cloud, formerly known as Storm, was quiet. Storm Attraction did not appear later. The two weather formations fought and rained. Cloud again upgraded to Storm. When extreme turbulence threatened to convert her into gale-forced winds, Mother Cloud rushed to apply storm insulation once more, and with a liberal hand, but it was no use. Winds increased.

The families whirled into each other, too. The winds all collided, overlapped, and ripped each other apart. After only a few short months the Merge Her exploded and dissolved into nothing.

Storm and Daddy Double HimACane were quiet for a while. Storm, Daddy, and Mother spent time picking up massively scattered debris in the echoing silence.

"We didn't know it would turn out like this," Mother Cloud said.

"We?" asked Storm weakly.

"Oh, I meant you, of course," Mother Cloud corrected. She headed off to Wind Shear Beauty Salon to tell all within earshot how "this breakup was so unfair to me…and all the costumes I chose were in such good taste….Storm's My Sight and of course EYE Space were well covered…and I, naturally, was charming…"

All three of them hid from themselves and hid behind smoke screens together in silence. Storm and Daddy soaked up Toxic Rain. Storm added Toxic Pellets when she could find them. Finally they resumed their lives as if nothing had happened. The sunset colors behind them faded to pastel and then became paler still. Color Fall was complete.

Chapter 6
Joy Full And Joy Fall

A new R.O.I. star appears, announcing a Resource-studded but black-and-white Double HimACane like Daddy and whose icicles look like Mother Cloud's, too. Storm, once again upgraded, pictures Little Clouds in her mind and assures Dim that he can handle all the Resources himself. After the Commit Meant, they first have a beautiful Her and then a handsome Him Baby Cloud. Dim Double HimACane becomes icier and Storm sucks up more Toxic Rain. She locates a Hidden Him for affection, but Dim suspects. Storm's Toxic Rain use produces unexpected Storm Surges in front of the Little Clouds. Dim inflames too.

The recent Color Fall produced fainter, monochromatic sunsets. Storm again took her place next to Daddy Double HimACane while Mother Cloud moved behind them. The three moved around as a unit in this formation. They protected themselves from each other and from outsiders by inhaling dust from Dust Devil Tubes and exhaling smoke screens.

Squinting through the Cloud family fog, Storm noticed spotlights in the distance. She puffed herself up and blew over to find the source. Local academies advertised for storm students. Ignoring Mother Cloud and Daddy's warning frowns, Storm bumped up to a Toxic Rain Cloud, filled herself up with Courage Us purple liquid, and entered Try Again Academy. She dropped out twice. Each time, she left when numbers were introduced.

Mother had told her many times, "We don't do numbers. You and I aren't made that way."

Storm hadn't asked questions then. She didn't this time, either. She contracted, blackened, and stormed away.

"Third time, you're out," she scolded herself. "Just stay home, Stay a Storm!"

Storm tried various jobs and spent time with assorted clouds and storms. She purchased HimACane tracking devices that included sophisticated HimACane Hunters. Even those failed to locate a potential mate. When she finally gave up her efforts, Storm felt the vibration of a gentle voice from within her center: "EYE M Vision and EYE M Hear. Let Me be the one to warm you."

Storm shook her head. She scanned the space around her with her Afraid-Are screen. "That voice must be coming from a HimACane attracted to me from somewhere nearby. I'll just ignore it for now," she told herself.

Daddy Double HimACane, tired from spinning around for Earth items, took a break. He left Mother and Storm alone to spend fun time collecting and hitting frozen raindrops from place to place with a partner he met on the frozen raindrops range. He later introduced this Him, a

Double HimACane like himself, to Storm, telling her, "He seems like a good fit for you for some reason."

Storm looked at him and gasped. His light seemed dim for a Double HimACane. His Earth My Sights were spotlights that created tunnel vision. Deep inside each tunnel were stored Earth Debris Resource items. Over his head hung a star, proclaiming "R.O.I." At first Storm smiled in delight at the name of her long-lost love, until she noticed the words beneath: "Return on Investment."

The sacred star degraded as it took on the color of the Earth Debris Resources. It looked like a twin of Daddy Double HimACane's star, only frostier and, well, dimmer. He appeared to be boxed, just like Daddy. He had a different sound around him, though, which wasn't Boxed Music but rather Music Boxed—he played the same few songs over and over and over. His My Sights looked uncomfortably familiar. Icy spears barbed his double wind masses, just like Mother Cloud's. His form revealed serious Ice Train. The light surrounding him reminded her of Mother Cloud when she took off her decorations.

Storm glanced up at Mother Cloud, who turned her head away slowly, then back again quickly. She studied Dim Double HimACane up and down, smiling. She turned to Storm and gave her "the nod."

Storm turned back to focus fully on Dim Double HimACane. His Cloud Bank was attached to him, and full of Earth Debris Resources.

"Yes, he has the double energy all right, just like Daddy. And he looks a lot like you too, Mother Cloud," whispered Storm. "But there's one problem. Everything around Dim Double HimACane is in black and white. He has no colors until he's near you or me when there's a reflection of us back onto him. And the space around him is in black and white, too."

"You'll provide the colors. He has power and a certain style, and that matters more," Mother Cloud hissed, while smiling toward Dim Double HimACane. "But of course it's your decision," she stated in a frosty tone, lifting her head and turning away. "You know your options at this point."

Dim nodded back at Mother Cloud and then turned to Storm. "I like your Mom's style," he said, his heavy clouds hanging low with unshed rain and ice. "And your Dad's, too!" He grinned at the close-up view of Daddy's twin funneled centers.

Something about Dim's energy seemed to keep her off balance. If she moved toward him, he moved away. If she moved away, he came closer. It seemed as if Boxed Music surrounded them quietly when this occurred. Storm lifted her head and smiled at that. It was a wonderful kind of Co-Depend Dance! She knew she could eventually win his love if she used enough Storm Attraction and My Will Power skills!

She moved in front of the sun and let it beam through the thinnest points in her cloud vapors. Using these borrowed spotlights, she briefly uncovered her My Sight—carefully keeping her deeper EYE Space covered, of course—and searched the sky. When Storm checked out her final options she saw again that to the left there was no career in sight. To the right there were no HimACanes that met her or Daddy Double HimACane's standards. Above her was a vision of getting older and being alone. Looking down she saw no mate, no children, and no power. Only obliteration, as her center would surely crack and open, and her clouds would thin out and vaporize. She patted down her layers to cover My Sight.

Her focused My Will Power produced a sudden burst of energy. She soaked up a large dose of Toxic Rain that predictably summoned up purple Courage Us. It suffused her center and lifted her effortlessly until she soared, seeming to rise above all obstacles. Storm roared through the sky with lightning, thunder, and gusty winds. Unfortunately, Over Expose Her occurred as the speed blew cirrus feathers away to reveal her My Sight. Stopping directly in front of Dim Double HimACane, she hastily fluffed cirrus cloud layers over this personal power and reshaped herself into a Little Cloud form. She attached some Storm Attraction for added interest. Dim received this combined display with focused, narrowed My Sights and a slight smile.

Storm's hard work to diminish and downgrade herself paid off. It wasn't easy this time, but she officially downgraded herself to a Cloud. Dim Double Him enjoyed her smaller size. He certainly liked her new name! At first Dim seemed to have Private My Sights. Cloud snuck up behind him in order to see *his* view for herself. The picture was quite clear. It was all about his R.O.I., or Return on Investment. Debris Resources were his Star, and he was focused on becoming Resource Full.

Cloud hurried to apply My Will Power, spending more and more time with Dim to attract him with Storm Attraction while staying Cloud sized. She accomplished this mixed message by first soaking up Toxic Rain. At these times Cloud predictably felt luscious warmth spread throughout her entire length. She felt her clouds expand into luxurious crests of loving rose and Courage Us purple, highlighted with unabashed gold. Then she purposely contracted herself.

She felt the switch, first inside of her and then between them as she and Dim Double HimACane smiled at one another in love and understanding. The air space around them blazed with color and glittered softly from his R.O.I. Impostar. She knew he was the right one!

Dim made a Commit Meant only after Cloud made a promise: She would let him be the only one who organized and doled out all the Cloud Banked Resource items in his tunnels. He sighed and smiled. She sighed and smiled too, allowing him to slip his special ring on her. Oddly enough, some kind of bracelet was attached. She Play Falled into Him. He caught her, but he didn't release her. Bars came into view all around her. She was trapped.

He lifted himself higher after this submission. He increased in size too, almost by two dimensions. He shone a pale light that permeated her empty heart. It was much lighter than Daddy's, but it felt somewhat cool, like Mother's.

In no time at all Cloud contracted further. The smaller she became, the greater the depth and dimension Dim Double Him seemed to acquire. Suddenly Cloud looked around and noticed some shadows darkening her surface. She gasped. Her My Sight opened wide, then her head dropped. How had this happened? She was in a golden cage, trapped and helpless.

Before long, Joy Fall increased. While storing and counting goods hidden deep in a Cloud Bank, Dim paused and straightened. When Cloud begged, he allowed her to listen to music. Even though the sounds were Music Boxed, Cloud hadn't minded, so long as he had let her listen. On occasion Dim Double HimACane even downed some Toxic Rain as he listened with her. Now he sharply pointed his hand downward toward the sounds. He lightning-zapped the energy transmitter. Silence.

"Music's over," Dim announced. "Time to grow up."

What was left of the surrounding pale colors ripped away. Mottled darkness with patches of tell-tale gray took their place. Black-and-white Expose Her caused Cloud to weaken and shrink even smaller. Her voice became much like the squeaky Little Cloud voice of former days, very much like Mother's.

Then a miracle happened. Make that two miracles! First there was a pink, then a blue tinge to the clouds—a sign in the sky. The dark clouds parted, slowly revealing My Will and My Dream of Baby Clouds on the way!

Cloud stared in amazement. "I'll love them so much and so deeply that I'll do everything right," she told herself. "I'll repeat the positive things that my parents taught me and absolutely won't repeat the negative things that my parents did." Her use of Dust Devil Tubes and Toxic Rain decreased and ended—for a while.

When Baby Her Cloud arrived, a break appeared in Dim Double HimACane's left My Sight. When Cloud mentioned it, he contracted his winds with My Will. His wind forces strengthened all around. Cloud's joy with this new little one was unparalleled. Sunlight cut through her darkness.

Next Baby Him Cloud appeared. Cloud glowed all over as she watched the sky change. When both arrivals were together Cloud thought she saw a break in Dim's right icy My Sight. He repaired it immediately, but he wasn't quick enough to catch a sparkling raindrop that escaped. Both Cloud Babies were beautiful. Cloud's Joy Full doubled. Joy Fall returned slowly. Cloud gasped when a passing Reflect Her Cloud pictured her as a young mother soaking up Toxic Rain at night and sucking on Dust Devil Tubes all day. Somehow she hadn't seen these behaviors returning.

"The very worst of both Mother Cloud and Daddy! How could it be?" she wondered with a sinking heart. "I have to use more My Will Power to stop this!"

But the more My Will Power she used, the worse it got. This was worse than strange. Depressed rain seeped into her center with an occasional Toxic Rain-induced runoff that produced no real relief.

For his part, Dim controlled all the Debris Resources and disappeared for long hours to play his game of Rainstones, a solitary version of the game he had played with Daddy Double HimACane. This game consisted of hitting around frozen raindrops that were poured or dribbled down from other clouds. He called these other expressive clouds "the plain clouds."

Cloud saw twilight turn to darkness each night she spent with Dim Double HimACane and his distant My Sights. When she tried to hug him, dry ice burned her or he simply blew her away. She soaked up Toxic Rain in greater and greater quantities. At unexpected times she whirled into Dim with fiery storms of inflammation produced from the Courage

Us liquid that she soaked up more and more. Under the influence of Toxic Rain power, she sometimes pounded away at his hardened surface without inhibition. Now and then she broke off a little of his ice. The Baby Clouds, watching in horror, covered their mouths and blew away in search of safety.

The next day Cloud quietly entered the main family area and once again noticed the Elephant in the middle of the room. Nobody, of course, mentioned it. Silent but quite large, this recurrent Elephant in the Living Room seemed like just one more thing she didn't understand. She carefully avoided it altogether. The rest of the family did too.

Over time even Toxic Rain failed to produce bonding with Dim anymore. The more she rained, the more he froze. The world became colder and smaller somehow. She changed her name to Storm again, then privately referred to herself as a Tropical Disturbed Dance. She sucked up the rain, thunder, and lightning and buried it deep inside so she could downgrade herself easily, returning to Cloud form.

But something was different now. She shifted back and forth from Cloud to Storm on a regular basis. She herself never knew what her name would be! One night she drank Toxic Rain, saw red, dropped low toward Earth, and bumped headlong into a mountain, causing a black My Sight. Her layers parted and all the neighbors discussed her obvious bruise behind her back. They thought Dim Double HimACane had caused it, for sure!

The next day the too-bright sun shone on Cloud, who had by then decreased in size and wasn't willing or able to move. She felt a locked-in emptiness in her center, with pain at the edges where full contentment used to sit a long, long time ago.

Dim Double HimACane's double vision tunnels withheld more and more items over time. He sprinkled a few from the top for Storm or Cloud, her name depending on when and how much Toxic Rain she had soaked up, and how it affected her on that day. Then he wheeled away to count his Cloud-Banked Debris Resources. He accused Storm, or Cloud, as he called her now, of always running out of basic items, no matter how she tried to save them. She alternated between upgrading and downgrading in response to his accusations.

With no other options in sight, Cloud tried to increase her Storm Attraction even more. She subsisted on crumbs to become smaller, prettier. All the while she drank more and more Toxic Rain. She indulged in sugarcane to relieve locked-in pain. The cold world around Dim produced Freeze Her Burn in Cloud, a painful combination.

One day she noticed a star hanging over a new Hidden Him on the horizon. It read, "Storm Attracted." The world was warmer as she approached it.

"Hmm," thought Cloud. "I'd fit that order. Maybe all I really need is someone to cuddle me!"

She upgraded herself to Storm once more and began to meet this warm Hidden Him to cuddle, or to hear him say she was special. Sweetness filled her emptied-out center once again. She got a tickly feeling in her tummy when she thought about meeting this new Him.

Somehow it seemed as if Dim Double HimACane knew about it. Once he spotted her returning home from the horizon. His My Sights blazed as he yelled, "Get home—NOW!"

She nodded her head. She slowly moved back toward the horizon whenever Hidden Him peeked out. Nothing more was said. If possible, Dim Double HimACane grew even more iced rain spears that hung from his form. Once or twice a year he started to sprinkle, but instead he froze and sucked it back up. "Who, me? I didn't rain. You're mistaken."

Daddy Double HimACane kept in close touch with Storm. He didn't much care for that name now, and let her know it. She gave him constant details of her ongoing and increasing distress. One day it finally reached a peak.

Daddy arrived with a purpose. He pulled hard on Storm's right side. "Your name needs to return to Cloud and Stay a Cloud! Get the Cloud Kiddies ready and come back home to live with Mother Cloud and me," he commanded.

Storm stayed still. She Stayed a Storm. Her layers spread out to the right.

Just then Dim Double HimACane appeared. He pulled on Storm's left side. "Get back in the house!" he roared. "You and the children belong to me."

High in the air the two Double HimACanes overlapped and then took opposite sides of Storm. Each pulled from one side of her and tried to overpower the other. To satisfy the two Hims, she Stayed a Storm in the middle and became Cloud on each side. Storm froze in place. Her layers thinned out. Her middle became transparent. A break formed in her center and she bent in half. She looked and felt like a wishbone.

"Please help me!" she begged the clear empty silence, her My Sight closed. Immediately her EYE Space opened wide.

"EYE M Vision and EYE M Hear," replied a voice.

Her My Ears perked up. She looked around. Seeing nothing, she shook her head and reopened her My Sight. As she did, the familiar voice from long ago became faint and then was heard no more.

Storm checked out her final options. In one direction, she saw no career in sight. Her dream of a family of four would soon be over. Looking the other way, there were no HimACanes to love her now. She could go back to live with Mother Cloud and Daddy Double HimACane, with no mate and no power. Her center would crack and empty, her clouds thinning out. It would be almost over. Obliteration.

Storm took a breath and withdrew her right side from Daddy Double HimACane. The released momentum yanked her well behind Dim Double HimACane and out of sight. Daddy reluctantly left. Even Hidden Him wouldn't be able to find her now.

Storm spent time working to cover her cracked My Sight. She plumped the area up with fluffy cumulus clouds. Still, the wound remained. A red cast flowed through, particularly when her Stormy winds increased to gale force. Trying to reason with Dim Double HimACane only intensified his agitation.

"I work for hours every day, rotating and churning better than any Double HimACane I know! My winds stir up more than enough to provide us with all a Cloud family would ever need or want! All you have to do is collect things! You should be grateful that I understand R.O.I., Return on Investments. You have no Resources of your own. You are the Her and I am the Direct Her! Just say, 'Yes, Sir!'"

Joy Fall intensified. Even with her My Sight wide open, she couldn't see anywhere else to turn.

Chapter 7
My Will and EYE Will

Storm finds herself facing Daddy's terminal illness from Dust Devil Tubes overuse. She whirls around and then back and forth between her Little Clouds with Dim Double HimACane and Mother Cloud with Daddy until she becomes a powerful HerACane. When Daddy is gone, she experiences such grief that she downgrades to Storm and then to Cloud. Without using Toxic Rain, she hears EYE M Higher Power for a few miraculous days. Then He seems to disappear. She regains whirlwind powers and HerACane status. Mother finds a new Him Cloud quickly. Eventually she has heart pains and obliterates from Earth too.

The beautiful Baby Clouds became Little Clouds. All the while nothing really changed until Daddy Double HimACane became sick with Dust Devil Clog. Daddy's double winds slowed down but held together. He threw away all his Dust Devil Tubes. He underwent Sun Ray treatments and soaked up a bit less Toxic Rain. Daddy was unable to stir up much Debris due to his weakened condition. He unloaded what items remained from his twin storage tunnels for Mother Cloud and himself, but Debris Resources were thinning out.

Storm overheard Daddy bargaining to trade items they possessed in order to replace the dwindling Resource supply. Mother Cloud looked small as she organized his things for him. Storm instinctively headed toward her mother with a queen-sized Comfort Her. She froze in place when Mother Cloud unexpectedly reversed course. All at once Mother expanded, reddened, and faced Daddy Double HimACane.

"Indian giver!" she accused Daddy. "You've traded away all my glitter rings!"

Daddy hovered uncertainly. His wind speed decreased alarmingly. Storm flew toward Mother Cloud. "How could you? He's sick, and you only care about tokens! And, Daddy, Mother Cloud will never grow up until you obliterate!" She clapped her hand over her mouth. She stormed away, raining all the while.

Storm spent the next months—which turned into years—calling various Dust Devil docs, propping Daddy Double HimACane up, and helping him trade away items for more Resources while Mother Cloud wasn't looking. Daddy became smaller and quieter and slower until he downgraded—first into a HimACane and then into a Him Storm. Then he decreased into a Him Cloud, hovering dangerously near land. He looked very white and small.

Storm, on the other hand, responded by unabashedly summoning up more My Will Power and strengthening into her new name: HerACane.

With much-needed energy, she moved back and forth from her own Little Clouds' home with Dim Double HimACane to Mother Cloud and Daddy and back again, over and over. Her winds circled around faster and faster. They howled. She was massive, empty, and Power Full.

Over time she whirled around in place without traveling. This was due to wind spin, a twirling condition resulting in the loss of the nutritious Feed Her Bands that she had never known she possessed and wouldn't have known how to use even if she had. She had looked outside herself to Mother Cloud and been told to Him Power herself. She had looked outside herself to Daddy's My Sight for her own source of peace and achieved movement only by riding on Daddy's back, or holding onto his tailwinds. She had accessed nourishment from *his* Feed Her Bands and never learned to feed herself. She had ignored her own decline and starved herself, body, mind, and spirit.

HerACane's whirlwinds overlapped and increased in speed. All this energy threatened to break her in two. A Double HerACane was on the way!

Mother interrupted this process. She called her to come immediately because Daddy, now barely a Cloud, could hardly breathe. HerACane roared over to find Mother Cloud straightening family costumes as if nothing was wrong. She didn't seem to notice that her Little Cloud, who had become Storm, had now upgraded to a HerACane. She pointedly looked away from Daddy. She did allow HerACane to pull her and Daddy to the safety of nearby Weather Support workers for emergency help. The workers took Daddy to a quiet airspace. Then they pulled Mother Cloud and HerACane aside, shaking their heads. Mother Cloud floated near, but not too near to Daddy.

HerACane took her usual place right beside Daddy, siphoning water droplets from a passing cloud into Daddy's mouth. Her winds slowed, churning in rhythm with his quiet breathing. He had thinned out and was almost trans-parent. His EYE Spaces had become clearly visible from deep within his broken My Sights. Still, he held on. At one point he looked at HerACane and smiled.

"What are you thinking about?" she asked.

"I'm remembering what fun your Mother Cloud and I had when you were little and we had only just enough Debris Resources and a house just the right size," he said.

HerACane saw the picture in her mind and smiled too.

After many hours, Daddy's winds slowed even more. Both of his My Sights released deeply hidden masks nobody knew he owned or used.

HerACane gasped. "Just like Mother's outer mask!" she whispered to herself.

Weather Support workers suggested HerACane and Mother Cloud leave for a while to give Daddy some Private EYE time. Spinning and filling herself with ineffective Toxic Rain, HerACane left. She pulled Mother Cloud along, raining all the way home. Mother appeared to be frozen.

When they returned to Mother and Daddy's home to rest and wait, Weather Support workers called with the dreaded news. "Your daddy is gone."

HerACane's scream could be heard for miles. Her rains, always ready to flow, froze in place for the first time ever. For several days she tried to move, but her first case of Dry My Sight held her quite still. She downgraded to a Storm and then a Cloud.

On the third night, she considered Toxic Rain. No, she didn't have enough energy to rise up toward an Anvil Cloud. She reached around instead for Toxic Pellets she had stored for this exact, intolerable event. Just before pressing them weakly into her folds, she heard a voice.

"Be still. EYE M Hear."

Cloud looked around, shaking. Nothing was there.

"Throw away the pellets. NOW."

Cloud complied. She watched as they fell down, down, down through the clouds to the ground below. She looked up and all around.

The voice continued, "EYE M Hear for you, now and always. EYE M Perfect Love."

Cloud felt a peace she had never known without Toxic Rain or Toxic Pellets seep into her and through her. It lasted for three heavenly days. It emanated from her center and spread all over her. On the fourth day it seemed to flow out of her. She chased the feeling with newfound energy. She visited cloud and storm groups singing and listening to praises of EYE M. She enjoyed the adventures and the music, but the peace was absent.

Had the voice been EYE M or was it really Daddy Double HimACane in his heavenly realm now, wondered Cloud. Over time, she sadly conceded it must have been Daddy. And now Daddy was gone. Whoever or whatever it had been, it was gone now. She gave up. She was on her own again.

She stayed with Mother Cloud for a time, trying to help her sort through Daddy's few remaining possessions. She returned to Toxic Rain evenings, increasing her intake due to the cracked emptiness in her middle from all her losses: Daddy Double HimACane, happiness with Dim Double HimACane, and now the loss of EYE M as well! She increased in size once again to Storm, then to HerACane.

Mother still showed very little reaction to the loss of Daddy. She reorganized, almost too fast, it seemed. She became smaller and icier and decorated her hook. She also redecorated her mask, adding glitter where much had worn off. Mother reached into a passing Him Cloud formation and immediately caught another Him. This one was a Him Storm, who had downgraded from a HimACane. The two of them listened to Boxed Music, told life stories, and took "naps." Mother Cloud contracted and giggled. She clung to his tailwinds. She even took the risk of floating alongside Him on occasion.

During one of his absences, she noticed HerACane's increased wind speed and movement. She demanded to know, "Why are you doing this to yourself? Your My Sight is obvious to one and all! Your EYE Space is almost showing! You promised us both that you'd Stay a Storm. You'll lose Dim Double HimACane to another female if you keep this up, and I really like him!"

HerACane got a small glimpse of Mother Cloud's My Sight. Mother Cloud's new Him Storm wobbled one day, thinned out, and disintegrated quickly. He obliterated. Mother returned to collecting Debris Resources as fast as possible, without looking up. Puffing energetically on the same Dust Devil Tubes that had ended Daddy's life, she turned to HerACane, head lifted high.

"You need to take care of me now. You need to take me places to collect more objects just as I'm used to doing. I deserve that. Find me more and more Debris Resources so I can live life as I always have. Let me hitch a ride on your tailwinds. Daddy would insist on it if he were here!"

HerACane's voice didn't sound like her own. "No. Mother Cloud, this behavior has gone far enough. You have to find something else to do now!"

"Then I just want to obliterate!" Mother Cloud threatened, reddening.

"But, Mother Cloud, why would you rather disappear than learn to live a different way? You don't need HimACanes and material objects to be happy. Since you just *refuse* to rain, maybe you can use some False Flow drops for moisture." HerACane offered the bottle slowly. "You'll feel better."

Mother Cloud frosted over. She backed away, darkened, and filled up with water. Her form filled up inside with more and more trapped liquid. "Whatever else happens, I don't want to rain."

HerACane watched as Mother Cloud shuddered. She didn't rain. Instead, she flash flooded from traumatized laughter. HerACane, for once in her life, stepped aside to avoid receiving Mother's distress.

"Daddy Double HimACane gave up. He let EYE M and EYE M Vision take over. He obliterated. It's ignominious," Mother stated firmly. "Look the word up for yourself in our copy of *Be Your Own Star—Brilliant Words for Great Ones!*"

Mother Cloud lifted her head, laughing hysterically. Then down came the deluge. Some ice chunks melted and fell. She froze them with My Will Power on the way down. Her My Sight edges cracked in half from the weight of it. Her outer clouds thinned out and vaporized. The inner mask she wore was revealed at long last. The harp she never played but carefully preserved within her folds appeared. It fell down, down, down to the ground below.

Just before Mother Cloud disappeared altogether, HerACane moved forward. She knew it was time to look closely at Mother Cloud's inner layers. It would be her only chance for Mother Cloud's Expose Her. HerACane held her breath.

Mother Cloud's final layer contained not one but two EYE Spaces! They were red, due to constant immersion in acid rain. They were embedded in solid ice, preventing EYE M Vision from appearing. They were as big—no—even bigger than Daddy Double HimACane's two EYE Spaces had been! She had kept the secret well and acted as if she couldn't see or move around. This was her way to secure Daddy's attentions. In truth, her Double My Sights had always been available for the status upgrade to a Double HerACane.

Mother Cloud disappeared quickly before her ice melted to reveal EYE M Vision. HerACane wailed for a long time but in a different way. After Mother Cloud's obliteration, she had no energy to locate Toxic Rain, nor to soak it up if she did. She fought sleep until it overtook her. When she awoke, she inhaled Dust Devil Tubes and immersed herself in Toxic Rain until she could hold no more.

Chapter 8

Step Up And Fall Down

HerACane learns that Dim Double HimACane has had a Hidden Her for many years. She decides to increase the HerACane power she's always sought and applies extra My Will Power and Toxic Rain. She becomes the potent Double HerACane of her dreams! To her shock and horror, her double whirlwinds separate from each other and threaten to implode on their way back together. In her terror she hears EYE M Higher Power's voice and obeys His instructions. She becomes Cloud again, experiences EYE M's presence, and converses with Him. He guides her to a Steps Ladder. After settling into a new way of life she falls down into an Eleck Trick Impostar. EYE M saves her once again.

A s she became saturated she considered her past. She had been called different names at different stages of her life: Perfect Cloud, Cloud, Storm, Stay a Storm, and HerACane. In between, she had encountered cold fronts, stationary fronts, and gale-forced winds. She had always craved the power that had been so elusive. She had wished for her own HimACane to take care of her. She had deeply yearned for HerACane-forced winds of her own. Oh yes, there it was. Now she remembered her secret, greatest dream—to acquire for herself the circular, doubled-wind forces that fueled her Daddy Double HimACane. My Will jolted her insides. She increased her My Will Power. Then she added more. What was it Daddy had said? "There's always room for more!" She closed her My Sight and tried harder with all the strength of her My Will Power.

She paused and listened intently. Her whistling winds increased. A Reflect Her mirror revealed a major change. She suddenly realized that her former names were all outmoded now. She had upgraded higher than before. Her new name was Double HerACane! Her smile lit up the bright blue sky. She had power! Courage! Control! DOUBLE My Sights! With My Will and My Will Power, she had achieved freedom. Her wish came true! My Will Power had strengthened her into an amazing double force!

She celebrated this monumental event by moving easily under one final Toxic Rain Cloud. A liberal dousing of that magical liquid soaked into the layers of each twin swirling energy form. Courage Us purple glowed outward from each center. The delicious burn of Toxic Rain lit up her My Sights and lifted her twin HerACane forms even higher in the sky. Double Vision had connected her to Double Power! Since her double winds had increased in power and speed in this long sought, twin funneled, spiral form, it was odd that she started to feel empty and weak again.

Then the horror began. As she traveled lower, near land and over open water, her vision changed. Each of her two HerACanes picked up so much wind speed that it veered out of control! Each one came so near to the other that they nearly crossed. Then they separated. One HerACane became stationary, whirling in place, while the other spun around and then roared off into the distance, leaving debris in its wake. Suddenly it returned, rotating straight toward its twin. Double HerACane had been taught that if her My Sights overlapped into Single EYE Space, she would obliterate. EYE M Vision would take over and all would be lost.

"No!" she screamed aloud.

Double HerACane realized there was no time, no way out, no way to avoid her own destruction. Obliteration. The end was near! She stared at the oncoming force.

"How can I control it?" she screamed into the atmosphere.

Silence answered. She screamed louder. "I have to do something!" More silence. Power Fall, Bliss Fall, Play Fall, Joy Fall, and Hope Fall zoomed toward her in an ever expanding black hole. Seconds before the two weather forces collided, Double HerACane looked right, left, down, and then up. She whispered, "I give up. I'm powerless. Please help me."

Then, from deep inside her, she heard a familiar voice. "Let go. *Relax on Impact.*"

She obeyed, releasing My Will Power. With that, her screaming winds diminished. The wayward HerACane roared into the still, relaxed, and trembling other HerACane. Instead of crashing, the energies overlapped. The two My Sights combined into one. The result was a single HerACane. She quickly diminished into a Storm and then a Cloud.

A pale blue butterfly appeared out of nowhere to support her. She was gently released into a soft, warm, billowy cradle of light. She focused on the Star, whose familiar blue light enveloped her on contact. R.O.I. Star revealed the presence of EYE M.

Now she remembered:

Wherever she went, however she moved, He was all around her. Perfect Cloud with EYE M. Warm. Protected. Loved. Forever and ever. Bliss Full. Perfect Love appeared, nourishing her with Feed Her Bands of pink. EYE M Vision and EYE M Hear took over. She returned to Perfect Cloud form. And she was still herself! She was still in one piece, but with new vision and new hearing. My Sight was simply replaced with EYE Sight. She could see more clearly, with more colors and more comfort. Earth hearing was replaced with EYE M Hear. She could hear the underlying tones and melodies in greater dimensions than before. Why, she wondered, had she fought this for so long?

The familiar blue light faded. Just before it vanished altogether, Perfect Cloud had to ask. "Wait! Please wait. Who are You and where have I seen You before? Please, will You tell me? I don't want to lose EYE M Vision and EYE M Hear!"

"EYE M EL ROI, the God Who Sees," the voice replied.

"EYE M, ROI, R.O.I.—where have You been? Why did You leave me just when I found You? I looked for You everywhere. I called You and You didn't answer," she whimpered, dripping Toxic Rain.

EYE M rinsed her off by dousing her form with a brief cleansing drizzle of rain. The shower felt warm and soft. "Perfect Cloud, EYE M never left. When you call, EYE M answers."

"Are You going to give me roses, entertain me, sing to me, and all those things I love, now that I found You-or rather now that I let You find me?" she asked.

EYE M smiled. "EYE M knows what you need. Your life isn't looking the way you really want it to. You're ready for something more practical. EYE M sending you back to where you left off. This time, because you're finally willing, EYE M will put certain others in front of you to guide you on your journey. If you remember to call Me sooner next time, it will be easier. It also helps to open your EYE Space to let Me in."

Perfect Cloud nodded. "I'm sure I'll call You. I have all the memories of Your incredible paradise right in my re-memory Cloud Bank. EYE M, why can't I be happy without Toxic Rain? Why did Dim Double HimACane choose a Hidden Her that soaks up even more Toxic Rain than I do? Why am I named Perfect Cloud only when I fall down to You? Why can't I see the way You see when I'm on my own without You? And what exactly is EYE M Vision and EYE M Hear?"

EYE M interrupted her with a hug. "More will be revealed when you're ready to receive it. I think it's time." He gently blew her up and away.

She followed a sign that led her toward a glowing ladder. She reached the first step, found real, authentic Courage Us at long last, and began to climb.

Soon Perfect Cloud heard a group of voices talking, laughing, and clapping. Shaking, but moving forward, she approached the assorted clouds, storms, and energies, expecting to be chastised for her out-of-control Toxic Rain behaviors. To her amazement, the weather formations engulfed her in handshakes, hugs, and greetings. Some were bigger than she, some smaller. All of them admitted they had the same problem with Toxic Rain. None of them had the power to control it. They actually celebrated that fact now! They celebrated Power Fall! Many of them wanted to know more about EYE M.

She hadn't imagined she would be willing to open that special place right in her center, especially with strangers. She felt luscious warmth spread throughout her entire length. She felt her cloud vapors expand into luxurious crests of loving rose and Courage Us purple, highlighted with unabashed gold. She had wanted to feel power, and now she realized she was happier without it. She gazed at the whole extended group of Support Hers. They smiled at one another in love and understanding. The rest of the evening passed in a haze of comfort and joy. Enlightenment appeared. The strangers, it turned out, weren't really strangers after all. The peace was beautiful.

"Keep coming back," they cheered her on as she left. "And have a Power Less day!"

Warmed into a buoyant, pink cloud of joy, she floated home. She hadn't remotely imagined she would feel this way: Warm. Protected. Loved. Bliss Full. Forever and ever. Home. Her gratitude to EYE M was profound. Hope filled her center with warmth.

Perfect Cloud found herself running back to Dim Double Him to give him the good news: "It's amazing! I found a miracle ladder that can set me free! I heard about a special ladder for you too, if you want it!"

She looked up at him and held her breath. He barely glanced at her and turned his head away. Her name and form returned to Cloud. The word Perfect had disappeared.

"I already have a ladder. I climbed my way to the top with more Debris Resources than most HimACanes stir up, and now I bank them up at the top." Dim lifted his head even higher than usual. "Umm, and as you can see now, I already have a new Her Cloud. We'll be making a Commit Meant soon. Good luck with your climb. Bye."

Cloud peeked over his shoulder to look. She pulled on a pair of Clear My Sight glasses. His focus was clear. A Debris Resource ladder gleamed within his vision. An increasing pile of Cloud-Banked investments rested at the top.

As Cloud turned to leave, she took a good long look at Hidden Her, Dim's choice of female replacement. She looked like Cloud's twin, only with more of it all. She was decorated and gulping hidden Toxic Rain hidden in her folds. She swallowed hidden Toxic Pellets, looking up at Dim with a certain blurry smile. Dim looked down on her, smiled slightly, and shook his head. In his folds was a new Commit Meant bracelet, an exact replica of the one he had secured onto Cloud. Yes, there was no doubt. These two were a team.

"She took my place!" sobbed Cloud, floating away.

Even with her new friends and the steps up the ladder, it didn't take long for Cloud to distract herself from EYE M, to feel empty inside again, and to look around for another Him to hook. She scanned the sky through suddenly Starry My Sight glasses.

A new Him arrived quickly, glittering and sending out fizzles. Cloud upgraded to Storm again and unfurled her special Him Hook. Closing in on her target, she was surprised to suddenly encounter *his* Her Hook. It fastened into her before she could make her own move. He grabbed her, pulling her close. He revealed that he too was a Storm.

He sprinkled her form liberally with mini-stars, tossing them into her layers like confetti at a party. She wasn't able or willing to focus on the sign displayed prominently in front of his weather system.

Storm climbed the My Fall tower and Play Falled into his folds and currents. She reeled with intense pleasure at the sights and sounds. He played Music Boxed and Boxed Music for her, fed her, tickled her, rubbed her, and sang to her. Best of all, he told her she was beautiful. He told her she had Storm Attraction. He called her Electra Cute too. He even called her "Perfect"!

Lightning flashed between them in ways that took her breath away. Storm vaguely remembered that she hadn't listened to or looked for EYE M in a while.

"Well, maybe that's okay," she told herself. "I have all the same feelings now that I used to have with EYE M anyway."

She remembered the way it was long ago:

She had basked in gentle, fleecy warmth. Saturated with Perfect Love, she sang songs radiating from her full, open heart. She moved to the beat in uninhibited joy. Tipping onto her back, she opened her mouth in sheer delight and blew sunrays up into the heavens.

EYE M shone His light on her with His sun by day. For twilight He painted sunsets for her in the neon pinks and vivid purples He knew were her favorites. He placed a vibrant yellow ball against a solid navy curtain to serve as her nightlight. He fed her the sweet love she craved. Perfect Cloud's joy was His joy. He decorated her with fragrant roses, dried her tears when she cried, hugged her, danced with her, and played special music for her ears alone. He entertained her with His voice, His art, and His theatre. He rained kisses on her. Wherever she went, however she moved, He was all around her.

All in One. Perfect Cloud with…with NEW HIM! Warm. Protected. Loved. Forever and ever.

One evening Storm had an itch. She scratched it. Staring at cottony hands, she discovered the mini-stars that had dotted her layers and her vision. Her Starry My Sight diminished. The Him approached her, tilting his head. He rotated her clouds, adjusting her form this way and that, frowning.

"You're 10 percent too small," he complained, pinching her. "Your form doesn't measure up. Maybe it would pass if we attached cotton balls here and here, but I doubt it."

Storm's Starry My Sight widened. Several stars lost their light as she flinched. "You said I was perfect just the way I was! Take these away. They're shams!"

She let the cotton balls fall down, down, down and out of sight. "Take them away."

Rain filled her My Sight, blurring the remaining stars inside. She backed up, sprinkled raindrops, and blinked. When her vision cleared she saw him in a completely different way.

He told Storm, "I'm the adorable one. You need to zip your mouth at all times. You're a Storm Object, and you know it! You need to Play Fall and do it my way or lose me altogether. Now slide down!"

His suddenly large middle girth and discordant music caused her winds to intensify, circulating in opposing directions around her. She grimaced. He sent a fizzle her way. It was different from before. It hurt.

She sent him one at the same time. The two combined, setting off fiery sparks that created mini-blasts. Small fires erupted all around them.

In desperation, Storm yanked on Starry My Sight glasses to return to her original Electra Cute vision. When these failed to provide relief she pulled on a pair of My Rose-Colored glasses. No luck. She could still see clearly.

Enlightenment struck her, leaving a raised and reddened burn. She screamed. With wide-open My Sight she moved forward to better read the words on the back of his Star: "Toxic Eleck Trick." Holding frost to her burn, sobbing and reversing into the night, she glanced at herself in a passing Reflect Her Cloud. She read aloud the star message hanging over her own head: "Electra Cute Shunned." She determinedly turned her head away from a nearby Toxic Rain Cloud. Then she desperately grabbed some Toxic Pellets just before they floated by her. She hid them in her folds. In a few minutes she shivered violently. Raining quietly, she allowed the Pellets to fall down, down, down to the Earth below.

She called for EYE M. She unfolded her cirrus ears for EYE M Hear and listened to His reply: Another Impostar. And once again you were the co-star. There's a deeper pattern of problems here. It's time for you to not only remember who you really were but to learn how to access who you really are and who you always will be. Let's send you to an emergency team of Seeing EYE Docs."

Chapter 9

Seeing EYE Docs

EYE M directs Perfect Cloud to three-dimensional support for communication and education. She allows her breakdown and begins to address recurrent relationship problems while two of the Docs deeply examine her Earth My Sights. As they explore aspects of her childhood, she's introduced to a different version of the life she thought was normal. She's shown a new perspective on her use of Toxic Rain and the dynamics from early childhood days.

But how will I recognize the Docs' office?" Perfect Cloud's winds spasmed.

EYE M shone a relaxing, blue spotlight over her through a passing cloud. "This spotlight will guide you to the EYE SENT HER. It's time to learn more about seeing Me—and hearing Me too. You'll find three Seeing EYE docs there. They each have a purpose. They'll know your name."

Naturally, it happened exactly that way. She was greeted by two of the three Docs, who presented themselves to her on their knees.

The second one spoke first. "Come in, we've been waiting for you! We're Seeing EYE Docs. It's a blessing to serve you. You must be Perfect Cloud. I'm Mind Doc, and the third in our trio is Body Doc. Our first Doc is...is..." He paused. "Well, you'll find out later," he said, smiling.

Sprinkling raindrops, Perfect Cloud took a deep breath, hesitated, and then moved closer. "How did you know my very first name? I've had so many. I started out as Perfect Cloud, a long, long time ago when I was with EYE M. While living near Earth I've been called Cloud, Storm, Stay a Storm, HerACane, and even Double HerACane." Her voice shook. "Now I feel Stormy again but but you're calling me Perfect Cloud. I don't know who I am anymore. Maybe I never really did. I think I'm having a breakdown. I'm breaking apart. I'm falling apart too!" She shivered, lost more altitude, and sprinkled raindrops.

The two Seeing EYE Docs smiled. Mind Doc, the spokesman, stepped forward.

"Ah. Only EYE M knows who you really are. If my hunch is correct, your My Sights have combined into one, are cracking up, and finally progressing to the breakdown that's necessary for the breakthrough," he told her. "Admitting your need for a good EYE Space cleaning beneath My Sight is really good news but probably doesn't feel too great at this point."

The two Seeing EYE Docs gathered together, looking closely at her partially revealed My Sight.

Perfect Cloud watched and listened intently.

"First of all," Mind Doc continued, "please remove these many decorations that you've used in your Electra Cute days to attract...well, various weather formations. You may keep your regular outer coverings on. Do you want to describe your symptoms in a sentence or two?"

Perfect Cloud followed instructions and took a huge breath. The Docs tilted their heads toward one another as they watched her and listened.

"Well," she began, "I'm Dis Him Powered. All my Hims are gone. I felt too Power Full with my first Him Cloud and then made a wrong promise with a Right Him and then made a right promise with a Wrong Dim Double Him, but had the right Baby Clouds. I felt Reject Shunned from Dim Double Him and snuck away with a new Hidden Him, and I just kept drinking Toxic Rain throughout it all and then said hello and goodbye to an Eleck Trick and came back, but found Dim Double Him with a new Hidden Her of his own, who was drinking Toxic Rain and swallowing Toxic Pellets too! And Dim Double Him won't stop seeing Hidden Her, who's not really hidden at all."

The Seeing EYE Docs blinked. They noted her verbal capacity with amazement.

She gulped some air and continued. "And my daddy was a Double HimACane, 'Le Roi,' French for king. He obliterated. And my mother, 'La Reine,' that's French for queen, just disappeared recently too, and—"

Mind Doc and Body Doc both interrupted. "And was he?" they asked in one voice.

Perfect Cloud tilted her head. "Was he what?"

"Was your daddy a king?"

Perfect Cloud paused and then nodded. "In a way, yes."

"And was your mother a queen? Low Rain? Did her rain hang low within her?"

"Um—to the first question, no, she only pretended to be. And to the second, yes, but raindrops did fall when she laughed hard enough. And that happened quite a lot at the very end. That's when I doubled My Will Power. I became a Double HerACane and celebrated that by soaking up lots of Toxic Rain. Then the unthinkable happened: One of my HerACanes turned on me and roared straight toward my other HerACane. Self-destruction!" Perfect Cloud trembled and contracted.

"And then what?" asked Body Doc.

"Well," Perfect Cloud said, her stressed voice becoming more peaceful, "EYE M saved my life through His R.O.I. Star, Relax on Impact. That's happened a few times now, actually. When I relax into the blue light under that Star, I seem to melt. A blue butterfly appears to support me. I see blue space instead of My Sight. EYE Space opens up. You called that EYE Space before, right? Then EYE M Vision appears. You called that EYE M Vision before. Right?"

Both Docs nodded, watching her passion suddenly appear.

"I become free, just like the white gull. I fly toward EYE M, who shows me where I want to go, which is kind of incredible but somehow familiar. I feel connected to Him! Finally, EYE M Perfect Vision arrives." She paused. "And I hear beautiful words and music too. It's brief, but no words can describe the beauty!"

Perfect Cloud continued. "This last time I stayed awhile with EYE M, and He led me to a Steps Ladder. I climbed it to live instead of obliterate, and then I stayed on the ladder to live without HerACane-forced winds or Toxic Rain. There are other weather forms there who became good friends, even a family of sorts. Now I don't soak up Toxic Rain—of any form—or inhale quite as many Dust Devil Tubes. I enrolled in Cloud Academy again too. I want to help others and share a vision that inspires them. I want to help them find EYE M, or at least their EYE Space, just like I've seen mine several times now." She turned her head away and then looked back at the Docs.

"But the problem of Hims still remains. After saying goodbye to Dim Double Ex, the father of my Little Clouds, I got hurt again—badly—by a new Him Storm. I didn't consider drinking Toxic Rain.

I did want to take Toxic Pellets, but I didn't do that. Being Dis Him Powered honestly never worked for me, not at all!"

She looked down at her thinned–out, transparent cloud band with the empty, heart-shaped center.

"When your Daddy Double HimACane obliterated and an accident threatened your existence, you released all the My Will Power that blocks you from EYE M," said Mind Doc. "This letting go dissolves Earth My Sight. It reveals clear, blue sky. If you stay there, the next stage occurs that announces EYE M Vision and EYE M Hear. Yes, it's the highlight of it all!"

Mind Doc sighed and continued. "However, for many, over time My Will Power builds up again. It's our job to help you understand why that happens. Oh, and about that first experience with Toxic Rain? It seemed as if you had found Bliss Full, just like when you were connected to EYE M. Yes, we know. It's the Impostar combination from Earth: Power, Resources, and So Much More Love. The ultimate three in one! But of course true Courage Us, security, and love don't arrive in a liquid or solid form to give instant relief."

Mind Doc leaned forward and spoke very directly. "The Steps Ladder you found is *very* important. You still need it. It's about 'we,' not about 'me.' Seek EYE M as you understand EYE M on that climb; it's a must. He leads you to us for even more freedom.

"It seems you've encountered the Earth Impostar called Power at close range, the pinnacle of your own self-willed Earth kind of strength. But instead of making you strong, you almost obliterated. Maybe the lesson was learned there—maybe! The concept known as My Powerlessness must be reviewed daily. That leaves you with two more Impostars—Earth Resources and So Much More Love—still sparkling and beckoning you near. They've become so painful now that you just might be willing to take a closer look. Power Impostar might still come into play there, so be aware!

"Unresolved childhood IMPs are no doubt floating around in your Earth My Sights. These are also known as family-of-origin issues. They continue to impair your vision and freedom, just as Toxic Rain blinded and blurred your world. The Impostar that promises So Much More Love dots your My Sights with heavy hearts until they're sorted and released. Oh, and please give us these extra Dust Devil Tubes you've hidden in your layers," directed Mind Doc.

Both Docs coughed and shook their heads while holding out their hands.

"We'll support EYE M in teaching you how to live without these things," instructed Body Doc. "It's all about unhealed relationships and using anger as protection. Open your Earth My Sight again now, please."

Perfect Cloud reluctantly reached out, releasing the smoky cylinders. Body Doc shone a light in her My Sight. "Hmmm…way too much Earth My Shadow, also called gloom and depression, along with virtually no Earth My Liner, also known as healthy boundaries. Some other Earth problems further down. Open wide…ah, just as I thought! Earth Pink I with Earth Black I deep down. This can cause blindness."

"I'm Earth Blind? How can that be, Body Doc?" Perfect Cloud shivered.

"Way too much reliance on Earth My Rose-Colored glasses. Let's just say your inner child is stuck in fantasy. There's a cover up at the top. You're seeing red. Inflamed. You're mad, in other words. Burning up, actually. And the Earth Black I? So many dark clouds are there that it seems like night. And you can't see at night. Tough situation." Body Doc leaned back.

"What can be done?" squeaked Perfect Cloud.

Body Doc sighed, looking into her other My Sight. "Your Earth My Sight is heavily defended by a reinforced EYE Wall. First of all, I'll need to dilate your My Sight to better check out your obstructed EYE Space. It will be uncomfortable but very necessary. Walls begin as a safety precaution in childhood and are also called survival skills. Children have little to no Earth My Liner. They're powerless, but not by choice. They must defer to their parents.

"Now please read these letters," instructed Body Doc, pointing to an Earth My Sight chart. He looked into her My Sights. "Yes. There are obvious Burn Her marks around the edges of your My Sights," he noted.

"True," added Mind Doc. "This indicates recent Expose Her to... ahem...a major Storm Attraction Disturbed Dance, probably a Him of some kind. I'm seeing the result of your use of Earth Electra Cute. You received quite a shock—an Eleck Trick! This latest Him, I'm sure, looked a lot like Daddy Double HimACane. How did it feel to break all the rules and trade zaps with Daddy for real? After all, isn't that the way it seemed Daddy was playing with your head all those years?"

Perfect Cloud gasped. "No, that didn't really happen with Daddy Double HimACane! We just had fun. He didn't touch me that way. Not exactly. Our relationship was more *special* than most fathers and daughters'. I probably just misunderstood. I'm his daughter, for heaven's sake!"

She turned red and paused. "I hate to admit this, but sometimes when Daddy seemed to prefer my company and admire my form more than Mother Cloud's, well...I kind of felt like...hey, great...wow...I'm winning!"

Her mouth turned downward. "My winds would move in a circle, first one way and then in the opposite way. I was kind of dizzy."

"Yes. Of course they would. And yes. Of course you were." The two Docs gave each other a knowing glance. Mind Doc spoke up.

"Let's rephrase that to say 'it was what it was' and you *thought* you were winning and you *felt* dizzy. More on that later. In any case, boundaries were absent in this situation, to say the very least. New information can be painful at first, as I told you."

Perfect Cloud broke in, "But it's my fault if I misinterpreted Daddy's attentions. I was just so special to him..." Perfect Cloud's form expanded slightly, and she lifted herself higher.

Mind Doc appeared unmoved. "Make no mistake, whether you liked it or not isn't the issue. Whether Daddy *physically* became intimate with you or not isn't the issue. We call this covert incest, also known as emotional incest. The operative word here is—"

"*Incest?*" gasped Perfect Cloud, dropping altitude quickly. "That's just wrong! That couldn't be true!"

"This in turn sets up an addictive response in future relationships," Mind Doc continued, as if she hadn't interrupted him. "Your identity became over-connected with your ability to attract Hims. You received a severe jolt of Electra Cute Shunned from your latest Impostar. You felt rejected at your core, just as if you didn't measure up for Daddy, your very first Him—a Double HimACane at that! Since Daddy never really belonged to you as a mate, he always seemed just out of reach. Ouch. You keep on trying to change that truth, over and over."

Perfect Cloud wrinkled her face, showing signs of fading resistance.

"I guarantee you wouldn't condone this parental behavior if it came from your ex toward your Little Her Cloud, right? Swimming without coverings together in the dark? Alone? And she's curvy now? Think about it." He looked directly into her My Sight as he spoke.

"Perfect Cloud, there were other special moments too, special backrubs in the dark. Just Daddy and you. And you were curvy by then, is that right? Don't shake your head. You can't emotionally leave home to be available for adult life or a mate until you admit to yourself what went on there. And there's more, right? *Special* lunches, *special* trips, *special* talks..."

"You're right. That's enough!" Perfect Cloud interrupted him. She nodded slowly, pink and red blotches appearing on her pale cloud face. Body Doc silently noted this physical reaction to emotional distress.

"Well, I forgive him then. He certainly wouldn't have done this on purpose to harm me. He did the best he could!" She turned her head.

"Not so fast," cautioned Mind Doc. "*Fast* forgiveness isn't necessarily the real thing. You haven't taken time to properly identify and feel the impact of Daddy's behaviors before releasing them— or releasing his accountability. You can't forgive what you don't fully know. Rather than authentic forgiveness, this can be known as emotional denial. The problem is, you have all the parental positive and negative impacts mixed up in your childhood suitcase. You can't tell the 'ahs' from the 'ows'—quite a mess! You haven't found the balance needed to release childhood and become your own parent."

Mind Doc made a sweeping, pointing motion to the side. "And where was Mother Cloud during this drama for two? Probably ignoring these events and sucking down her feelings, adding to her accumulation of Low Rain. La Reine, her fancy new name, usually brought up the rear behind you and Daddy, unless I miss my guess."

He paused and then nodded. "It seems Mother encouraged early relationships between you and Him Clouds in order to divert you and regain her mate's attention. That way she could become special, Number One with Daddy again. This was bad news for you, her need to compete with you instead of to protect you. Along with early stimulation from Daddy, this was a setup for behaviors that would bring you shame later on. Am I right? Against your instincts, you also agreed to copy Mom's costume and never felt comfortable enough to take it off and find your own look, did you?"

Perfect Cloud floated in stunned silence.

"Do you have a picture of Mother Cloud?" prodded Body Doc. When she brought one out of her folds to show him, he whistled. "Ooh. Nasty Ice Train. And there's a picture of Dim Double Ex."

"They look like twins!" the two Seeing Eye Docs exclaimed together. "And this one of you! You look just like your Mom!"

Mind Doc regained composure and cleared his throat. "Just so you know, you're not alone with the Electra Complex. In other cases it can be a little Him who 'dates' his mother for way too long, without the natural boundaries imposed by a healthy Daddy Him. In that case the same unhealthy dynamic—the opposite of the Electra Complex—can develop, called..."

"The Octopus Complex?" suggested Perfect Cloud.

The Seeing EYE Docs smiled. "Close. It's called the Oedipus Complex."

"Okay," Perfect Cloud agreed. "But wait! Back up a minute. First, how did you know Daddy had special swim time with me and special backrubs with me? I didn't tell you! And who are you and Body Doc talking to when you look up, listen, and nod? Nobody's there. I thought I heard something too, but if you can't see it, it's not really there."

The two Docs shrugged. "That's called reliance on Earth My Sight, with a complete lack of EYE Sight. Fear not. More will be revealed. It always is."

Perfect Cloud continued. "The most obvious things about Dim Double Ex besides his double winds were two spotlights from two My Sights and spikes of frozen water trailing from him too. What did that mean, Body Doc?"

"Hmm. Tunnel vision along with Ice Train. Dangerous combo. Everyone needs to rain every now and then. It's normal. Rain that's never expressed hangs down, eventually freezes, and over time you have the infamous Ice Train dragging from behind. Your Mother Cloud, Low

Rain, or, pardon me, La Reine, would know about that too. Hanging onto or moving around with either Mother's or Dim's frozen energies would definitely cause loco motion!"

"Oh, it did. And, Mind Doc, when Mother Cloud laughed, she sometimes rained. It was really strange rain. It kind of burned when it touched me."

"Acid Rain is full of stress-filled venom, that's why. At least her feelings were finally able to melt the ice and drain a bit."

"...and Dim Double Ex hardly ever rained. He burned me with his words," Perfect Cloud said.

"Not surprising that it burned. Dry Ice is the most potent Freeze Her Burn," explained Body Doc.

"Docs, all I know is, I rained a lot. And I drank a lot of Toxic Rain."

"Toxic Rain? That was an addiction on your part, for sure. Expressing feelings only through rain? Him freezes over, Her floods the city!" Body Doc smiled. "You see his low light as 'Dim' and he sees your high light as 'Dumb'! You see his black and white as 'I feel trapped' while he sees your up-and-down explosions as 'I feel zapped.'"

Mind Doc added, "You ignored the problem and found a Hidden Him. He ignored the problem and found a Hidden Her. At the time you chose each other, you were 'right' for each other. Now you're both 'wrong'—for each other, that is."

Perfect Cloud nodded and continued. "Dim also had a constant focus on an R.O.I. Star—but it turned out to mean Return on Investments for him; he focused on storing and saving those Resources almost as much as I focused on soaking up Toxic Rain! 'Save, store, save more!' he yelled. I finally yelled back, 'Use! Use! Use!' Which one of us was right?"

She interrupted herself and frowned. "Daddy and Mother both acted differently when Daddy Double HimACane stirred up more and more Resources. There's something wrong with having all those Debris Resources, right? Life was so much better when Daddy and

Mother had only a few of them. In large quantities they seem to cause harm to everyone."

"Hmm." Mind Doc followed her thought to its core. "Balance is always the key. Of course, anything you choose to put on a pedestal is a problem in the making. There's only One who's worthy of a true pedestal. And of course that One doesn't need or want a pedestal. At times a podium might be nice, though." Both Seeing EYE Docs shared a grin.

Perfect Cloud raised her brow in confusion.

Mind Doc turned away from her, carefully studying a piece of this Earth Debris Resource. "I don't see anything wrong—or even anything right with this item."

From the invisible realm there came a solid "True."

"Of course," he added, appearing not to notice her response, "it's what one thinks about it that's important. Thinking 'I need more and more' or 'there's never enough,' and identifying oneself as special or unworthy is the hook. Overemphasis on anything can lead to addiction. Black-and-white thinking, all or nothing, doesn't leave room for the middle, called the gray area. Balance is the solution to Debris Resource addiction, along with gratitude for 'just enough.' Like the Impostars named Power and So Much More Love, it's empty inside. Focus on the Real Star."

Perfect Cloud considered for a moment. "Maybe I'm just not seeing Dim Double HimACane right. He and Daddy Double HimACane and Mother Cloud all said I don't see things right. Maybe I just need new My Rose-Colored glasses."

The two Seeing EYE Docs leaned forward. "Okay. Great. There's a plan!" said Mind Doc, his voice surprisingly sharp. "When you return to fantasy vision you can see with magnified *distortion*. Your faulty Earth My Sight is then *reinforced* with a wall that you've built to protect yourself from seeing the real truth. All of that is then supported by your

My Will Power, which tells you that you can do everything on your own, all by yourself. *Maybe* I just have to keep trying harder, you tell yourself. How's it working for you so far?"

"Not very well," Perfect Cloud admitted. She giggled. "And just then you sounded like another doctor we all know."

"Correction," stated Mind Doc. "That doctor sounds like us!" All three shared a smile.

"So at this point, sharing your inconsistent ability to access EYE M Vision while still stuck in My Sight, which favors Earth Vision most of the time, probably won't help others much. Helping them locate anything at all would be 'the blind leading the blind.' In other words, you can't give to others what you don't securely have for yourself yet."

Perfect Cloud straightened out her form and deflated down to right size.

Chapter 10

Impostar Burst

Body Doc steps forward with a detailed inspection and discussion of Perfect Cloud's upgrades and downgrades into Storm, HerACane, and Double HerACane forms. He explains her various colors and physical reactions to external events. Mind Doc joins in, further connecting her childhood messages to her adult behaviors. He illustrates anger as an umbrella emotion and teaches her to identify feelings beneath the anger. He reveals the connection between childhood pain and adult relationship problems. Perfect Cloud becomes so fascinated with the two Docs that she refuses help from the third one.

"**A**nd an FYI: Single Vision from the Perfect Inner Sight of EYE M shows more clarity and truth than Double Earth My Sights," said

Body Doc. "Less is more in this case. Why? Because My Strain is very real, but EYE Strain doesn't even exist. It's the same thing with sound. Single Sound from the Perfect Inner Ear of EYE M also gives true hearing better than Double Earth My Ears. The most powerful thing to do is to allow your own powerlessness! Let EYE M see *and* hear for you, period."

Both Docs stood back and watched her reaction. Perfect Cloud nodded but also had a question. "Will you tell me why my form goes back and forth between little and big? I also change colors. My name keeps changing then too!"

Body Doc stepped forward. "Ah, my turn! Now we're discussing the impact of emotions. Let's talk about expression versus depression. Depressed feelings are black—dark as night. No sun can get in for very long. All anger that isn't broken down into identified feelings contributes to various physical diseases."

Body Doc continued, assuming a mean face mask. "For instance, anger is a secondary emotion. It's the only emotion that isn't a first, vulnerable feeling, but a buildup of smaller, cloudy feelings pushed down and stuck. They each have specific names. Warm, sad, lost, worried, hurt—these are just a few of the cloudy feelings that can be left unattended.

"The best way toward relief is to allow the feelings to be named, felt, expressed, and released. Your inner child would love to do that for you—if you let her! If you resist them, the feelings build up inside into a need for protection, for power. That anger will rise up, waiting to over-express in outbursts of rage, or be sucked down into depression—that's anger without enthusiasm—or burst out sideways as passive aggression. That one really stings! It just isn't honest, either." He shook his head.

"What about taking a Magic Pellet so that only happy feelings can come in?" Perfect Cloud asked, beaming up at the Docs with an instant answer.

The Docs looked at each other and tightened their lips. Mind Doc spoke. "Those pellets do exist, and might help in certain cases, but they're really meant to bring you to a state to receive emotional education and to practice with me. That process takes time. Too much pellet reliance without emotional education creates a lack of feelings altogether. Then we call them 'anti-expressants'! You just feel FLAT."

Perfect Cloud nodded and sighed.

"Both thoughts and feelings contribute to the physical form's state," inserted Body Doc. "Changes occur as a physical response. Big, little, dark, bright, red, black, pink, or white. Upgrading or increasing in size is an act that assures you you're greater than others. You then assume larger proportions to keep up the façade, or fake size, so to speak. Inflated ego known as pride. When you downgrade or become smaller in size, you tell yourself you're less than others. You're worse than anyone. Deflated ego known as shame. Both are ego extremes. Neither tells the truth. You're not greater than others, and you're not less than others. You're one of all the others—special, just like they all are. But what's needed is right size: humility."

At their next meeting, Mind Doc gave her more details. "Healthy parents help the child, not by imposing their personal form of Boxed Music onto them, but by exposing them to all music and helping them to recall their own special music that lies within. They strive to hear EYE M's voice and see through EYE M Vision themselves in order to better guide their child. They learn to communicate intimately by sharing their thoughts and feelings and teaching the child to do the same."

Mind Doc continued. "Most parents are unaware of all that. Unhealed Impostar love doesn't appear either loving or forgivable. It blocks the natural flow. Those emotional wounds don't disappear as a child becomes an adult, but rather remain as floaters in Earth My Sight, waiting to be healed. That work takes Courage Us, and not the kind you soak up from Toxic Rain Clouds!"

Perfect Cloud nodded too energetically and turned to move away.

"Wait a minute." Mind Doc's tone of voice stopped her. "Not so fast. How do you feel?"

She swiveled back toward him. "I *feel* that I should leave—now!" She raised her head, expanding in size.

Mind Doc corrected her. "That's a thought, not a feeling."

She contracted a bit.

"Let's say you *think* I'm asking you to make changes that are new and you *feel* anxious, uncomfortable, and trapped. See?"

She reluctantly nodded, returning to right size and trembling a bit.

"Okay, more on that skill later. Now let me finish. I know it's a lot to learn, but you'll need it all. After you've acknowledged the mistakes and hurts from those childhood years, along with the positives of course, you will realize you were held hostage to the family system as a child. You continued to hold *yourself* hostage because you didn't sort it all out and learn to parent yourself as an adult.

"Then you in turn held your own Little Clouds hostage. Until there's an intervention, this continues for generations. Little Clouds know deep inside that they are helpless to fend for themselves without the love and care of the family of origin. Therefore, they will do whatever it takes to accommodate that family system. They will even rename love as whatever the family says it is. This can become quite twisted. Everything from taunting to abuse to addictions can be reinterpreted as love." Mind Doc paused briefly. Body Doc stood nearby.

"Many addictive behaviors begin as a family form of love in a dysfunctional home—one in which the parents are not in touch with feelings and thoughts and don't allow EYE M to guide them. In fact, they usually become controlling and try to take EYE M's place altogether. Many are trained in childhood to ignore the large presence of a certain Elephant."

"Oh I know that one!" interrupted Perfect Cloud. "The White Elephant, right? No, that's a gift nobody wants," she corrected herself. "The Pink Elephant? Yes, that's it!" She clapped. Then she realized her mistake. "No, that's when someone is told not to think certain thoughts, like picturing pink elephants, and then the thoughts actually increase. I give up. What Elephant do I need to name?"

"The Elephant in the Living Room," chorused Mind and Body Docs.

Mind Doc continued to explain. "Children learn to pretend the problem isn't really there, even though, like an elephant, it's obvious and big and—just like that animal's presence would be in a living room—inappropriate. Children learn to mistrust their instincts and tell themselves their feelings are inaccurate or somehow wrong. The family refuses to assist by acknowledging the truth, either due to feelings of pride, shame, or fear. So nobody will name it, claim it, and feel it. They stay in the problem while refusing to admit it's a problem. So no solution!" Mind Doc stopped, giving Perfect Cloud a chance to reflect.

"Over time, each child learns to love the comfortable discomfort provided by that certain Elephant in the Living Room. As they get older they find friends, mates, or even jobs that subconsciously repeat the family-of-origin situations that are uncomfortable but strangely familiar. The Elephant symbolizes 'Don't be honest, don't be authentic, don't be who you are. Keep the family secrets.' This is also known as false shame.

"We all know about your repeated use of Toxic Rain," Mind Doc told her, looking into her My Sights. "It felt like liquid love, until it turned into pain and humiliation. It felt like Courage Us, until it twisted you into a coward, afraid of life itself. It seemed to fill that empty void, as all good Impostars must. Let's take a closer look at a few of the other addictions."

He continued. "Food is a necessity. It sometimes twists into an Impostar reminiscent of family love. Consider these other addictive behaviors and the shape they took. They all began with Hidden Hooks:

Toxic Pellets, Sleep Pellets, Dust Devil Tubes, Debris Resources for bartering and trading—and even the various forms of sugarcane!"

Perfect Cloud nodded slowly, with tight lips.

Mind Doc pointed to the addictions menu nearby. "See the one that looks like a fishhook heart? It's attached to the Elephant in the Living Room, one of the most difficult Impostars to unhook from because it's the most magnetic: relationship addiction. It's the second layer and is underneath all other addictions. When left untreated, it results in either the love avoidant or the love addict. That relationship is a Codepend Dance; come here, go away! Each mate has two fears: fear of intimacy and fear of abandonment—in opposite orders.

"The hook is called Tox Sick Love Trick. This dynamic is the *repetition compulsion*, or an obsession to receive your unmet childhood needs from an adult mate—you and your mate hook into each other and function as either the parent or the child. It feels really good...until it doesn't. 'Oh goodie, I'll finally get what I needed from Mom and Dad!'...or 'I'll have Mom and Dad power over someone!' This can end with 'you're hurting me all over again, Mom and Dad!' It's much harder to disengage from this than you might think," he added, frowning.

"If I keep doing this over and over, then my childhood will change, even though it's over' is not the thinking of a sound mind but the warped belief from a child's determined heart. Yes, that child still lives inside the adult. To break free of these and other behaviors, you need all three Seeing EYE Docs, a Steps Ladder, and much support. You'll also need to accept that childhood is over, that you're an adult and no longer 'one half' of anything, needing to find your 'other half.' You become whole and empowered. You're then available for another who is also whole and *em*powered—not *HIM*-Powered or *HER*-Powered." He frowned at her again in a way that also seemed like a smile.

Perfect Cloud squinted up at Mind Doc and sighed.

"Perfect Cloud, let me illustrate this for you in terms of birds. As a Little Cloud, you loved seagulls, right?" She nodded, smiling. "The color white symbolizes the innocence at your very core, then *and* now. A healthy family of origin gradually redirects little ones from dependence on them to dependence on EYE M. They do this by redirecting them and by helping them access their EYE Space. Gentle movement, called flying and flowing, is then created from the power that EYE M *would* never and *could* never abuse. Your future mate will honor your relationship with EYE M because he'll have one too."

"Yes, that makes sense!" Perfect Cloud's enthusiasm caused her winds to dance.

"Let's summarize the problem here." Mind Doc straightened up and continued. "You've been avoiding Toxic Rain and seeking EYE M's presence. You've worked to clean your My Sight so you can see through EYE Space with EYE M Vision. But your vision is still so obscured, or triggered, that old issues are still floating around, clouding your vision. You're living in the past and can't see the present. You're all about 'Me! Me! Me!'—followed by an occasional 'My!' This makes your world quite small and mainly all about you-know-who. It's hard to help others when you're literally stuck—stuck on yourself."

Hearing this, Perfect Cloud smiled a guilty smile.

Mind Doc continued. "Your vision is so obscured that you've been finding Toxic weather patterns instead of the real Power Source. Your adult self is your intellect. Your little inner child is your emotion. This fraction is the empowered adult—the decision maker overruling the feelings, while considering them as well.

"But when you've stuffed and ignored emotions for so long, they get bigger and bigger—picture a little kid pulling on you to get your attention and getting louder and louder. What you resist persists! Now we have emotion over intellect. The child is in charge of decisions. Uh-oh. Reactive, not proactive! Eventually, if the inner child never speaks at all, the stuck feelings cause whirlwinds—not really power at all, just trapped, de-pressed, unexpressed energy. Freedom of movement can only occur after the feelings are named, felt, expressed, and released."

Perfect Cloud nodded and left to think it all over. The next time they spoke, she was ready for more.

"If you want to do something different, you have to learn something different," Mind Doc reminded her. "Otherwise you only go around in a circle, going nowhere. Ever heard of doing the same thing over and over again, while expecting different results?"

Perfect Cloud frowned. "Hmm, yes, I think so. Isn't that called stupidity?"

"No, not really. Insanity is a bit different from that. You've heard of Wind Spin?" the Mind Doc continued. "As you repeat your efforts, the winds strengthen and debris is hurled at others from the momentum, hurting them. This is an example of—yes—insanity. This is definitely not of a sound mind. The likelihood is that you'll continue getting caught up in the black-and-white Wind Spins of others you attract. The pattern will continue. You need a plan to get out. Then you need to change your choice of associates! This isn't judging others; it's applying discernment. Decide on what you will and won't allow. Then reveal that and take care of yourself based on the response you hear from the other. This is called a boundary."

Perfect Cloud nodded.

"You've been trying to access the sweetness that feeds your life from external sources that wear out or leave. Now it seems the sugar you have left is drained out or locked up. And the natural defense from pain— the sweet love source—appears gone. In other words, you're running on empty. These sugar substitutes are known as Impostars because they only work briefly and end up leaving a bitter taste."

Hearing this was too much for her. Perfect Cloud put her hands over her Inner Ear. She turned and grabbed some sugarcane floating by and munched on it intensely. "But I need sugar inside me! It seems like it's all gone most of the time."

Body Doc intervened by grabbing the sugar. Mind Doc moved very close to her, held her hands together, and pointed to her heart-shaped center. "But the sweetness you need is right there! It's always been there. You can't see it with your My Sight.

"You need a HerACane Relief Plan. It's time to drop the ego walls, build some healthy fences, and go deeper than your outer form. Storm Attraction can only get you so far—mainly in the wrong direction, to be treated like a Storm Object." He made a face. "Now it's time for the solution. You can learn to parent your inner child." He paused, looked up, whispered into the air, and nodded. "Then you'll have a choice. You can really allow EYE M, your Create Her, to lead the way to freedom. You can be the Co-Create Her, Co-Star of the real Star and Free Flow. Then, and only then, will you have the right or the capability to inspire others. EYE M offers the sweetness that doesn't lock up or seep out."

Perfect Cloud sighed. "I believe you, but all that sounds really complicated to me. You're both sure EYE M has a vision for me?"

"You bet," chorused Mind Doc and Body Doc. "We'll all have work to do!"

Perfect Cloud discovered it was indeed hard work to "let go," a strange state of affairs. It wasn't always fun to feel with her inner child. Sometimes she rained or thundered for too long and needed help to return to her adult, parented state. She used her natural persistence to good end, though. Soon she was able to distinguish between thinking with her intellect and identifying and feeling her emotions. Her own empowered intellect over emotion—the parent and child of herself—began to work as a team. Some walls came tumbling down. She practiced empowerment."

Body Doc and Mind Doc celebrated in stereo. "Now you're ready for more!" they declared.

"I don't know how my inner child *feels* about that," Perfect Cloud said, half smiling.

"Very funny," commented Body Doc. "More My Sight work coming up here. We're a team now, you and us Docs. We've noticed your tendency to pick mates—and friends, for that matter—who remind you of Mother Cloud or Daddy Double HimACane, right? Unfortunately, this is emotional. You haven't chosen the positive qualities from your parents, but rather the more negative ones."

Mind Doc pointed out, "At least your Mother Cloud and Daddy Double HimACane had a Boxed Music dance in the beginning. You and Dim Double Ex never got that far. The music was frozen within you both. My wish for each of you is that you experience true love born of Inter Depend Dance with another. What you had was a Tox Sick relationship, not unlike the Toxic Rain of old. And it's not the parent in you who was doing the picking here! It's the inner kid."

Perfect Cloud bobbed her head up and down in agreement.

"This child believes she somehow failed if her parents weren't available to meet her emotional or physical needs. She's determined to somehow 'do better' this time, repeat the childhood dynamic and receive a different parental response," Mind Doc said. "If the child felt overpowered and abused or smothered, it created teenage-style walls to oppose but stay connected to its childhood parent. Rebellion. If the child felt insecure and overlooked or abandoned, it continued to try to 'please' its childhood parent.

"The inner child clings to the notion that it can make everything turn out the way it never did—and never will. This repetition compulsion is subconscious, persistent, and destined to fail from the start," explained Mind Doc. "It's a setup for you to become quickly overly infatuated and then to reject the other—or be rejected. Kind of the 'come here, go away' dance. Childhood's over. It's time to reparent yourself."

He leaned back, grinning broadly. "If we do this right, you'll be attracted to an empowered mate, not a parent or a child, the next go-around!"

Perfect Cloud let out a cheer. Both Docs clapped and smiled at her.

"There's your enthusiastic feeling, your gift expressed! Great! Everyone's feelings are RIGHT all the time. Emotional connection is us! That's because feelings are produced by the thought, which is of course one's response to an event. Now reframe the situation, become the parent of yourself in the present, and *voila*! You've cut the cord of childhood a bit more. Then you can really embrace adult life without the triggers of family-of-origin issues known as—remember? *Relationship Addiction*. What you think, and then what you feel, begin as a fact. They end up as a choice."

Perfect Cloud looked confused.

Mind Doc tried again. "Have you ever heard of Albert Ellis? He was quite an outstanding Mind Doc who introduced the A-B-C Theory, which says A) equals an event, B) equals my thought about the event, and C) equals my feelings. This becomes my reality. An event, any event, 'is what it is,' which assumes you have the freedom to consider the event from different perspectives and decide what to think. It's a choice. That freedom, though, can only come after you deal with your triggers and unpack that childhood suitcase. Then I'll help you reparent yourself with Fritz Perls' Gestalt therapy to emotionally leave your childhood ow's, bring forward your childhood ah's, and *really* live in the present. You can create the new too! That's the ultimate goal."

He lowered his voice and raised his eyebrows in an exaggerated arch. "Then it really is what it is, and not what it used to be!" All three shared a laugh.

Both Seeing EYE Docs stepped forward and looked at her directly. Then they turned away and looked up again at something or someone that Perfect Cloud couldn't see. They spoke to her in unison.

"Relaxing your My Will Power will empty and crumble your overprotective My Wall and finally allow the entrance of the Third Doc. He's a special Seeing EYE Doc that accesses EYE M Vision. His name is Spirit Doc. He'll help you find all you'll ever need, your true power, your *intuition,* which is—"

"Which is you! I already found my *inner wishin'.* I was inner wishin' for both of *you!*" interrupted Perfect Cloud, her My Sight suddenly open wide, obscuring EYE Sight and once again rendering her unable to see the truth. "I can't see the Third Doc, so maybe He's invisible and not even here, but it's absolutely okay!"

"But wait," cautioned the two Seeing EYE Docs in their new combined, dimensional voice, as Perfect Cloud's adoration raised them higher into the air. They left their modest platforms and rose—rose against their will—rising higher onto a pedestal. They cupped their hands into megaphones, calling down to her in a voice of desperation.

"Just be still and focus with your Single Inner EYE Space! Take some time to open your Inner Hear! Yes, you'll see and hear Spirit Doc...just take the time to meditate. Allow the EYE Space needed for Spirit Doc to appear. Release your My Will through the process. You need to offer your will to EYE M. Remember how Bliss Full that feels when you're Power Less and He's Power Full? It's a process, not an event. Please... We'll disappear from sight if you force us up too high and refuse to even meet Spirit Doc! He leads to EYE M Vision. EYE M wants to create a relationship with you. He needs your full attention!"

The two Seeing EYE Docs focused on My Rose-Colored glasses that reappeared out of nowhere and floated dangerously near to Perfect Cloud. As the glasses approached her, the Docs' voices began to fade from her Earth My Ear.

Perfect Cloud continued with her new train of thought. "Well, Spirit Doc can just take My Will from me when He wants to, or—." She had a sudden inspiration and returned with a spray bottle. "Instead of soaking up Toxic Rain or inhaling Dust Devil Tubes, I can just spray this Will Away on My Sights and My Ears to remove My Will. It's immediate relief. See?"

She sprayed this concoction all over herself. The Docs noticed that no change took place. She yanked her My Rose-Colored glasses back on. My Sight returned. Fantasy, denial, the Earth My Sight from childhood, all took over once again.

"Do you know how wonderful you two are?" she called up, arms outstretched and My Sights wide open. "You two Seeing EYE Docs are unbelievably amazing teachers and guides. Yes, we're a team. The parents I always wanted! Perfect Love! I want to be with you forever, Mom and Dad!" she exclaimed, fanning out and looking up in the opposite direction from Spirit Doc.

"You are...you are both absolutely brilliant! The shiniest Stars of them all!" she breathed. She glowed up at them with worship, truly believing they deserved those words she remembered so well:

He decorated her with fragrant roses, dried her tears when she cried, hugged her, danced with her, and played special music for her ears alone. He entertained her with His voice, His art, and His theatre. He rained kisses on her. Wherever she went, however she moved, He was all around her. All in One. Perfect Cloud with Seeing EYE Docs. Warm. Protected. Loved. Forever and ever...Bliss Full.

She blinked and held her arms out to...to nothing. There was silence.

The two Seeing EYE Docs had blown up and disappeared. She was alone. Lost. Abandoned again. Rejected. Shunned. Bliss Fall.

Chapter 11

My Will Or EYE Will

EYE M arrives to comfort and to confront Perfect Cloud. He emphasizes the need for Spirit Doc and says that He is the most important of the three. He urges her to practice what she's learned but to find balance when dealing with others to avoid idolizing or rejecting them. He reframes Mother Cloud and Daddy Double HimACane's behaviors throughout their childhoods. He offers an explanation that doesn't minimize the impacts on Perfect Cloud but provides balance. He mentors her in the stages necessary for true forgiveness.

S he looked left and right. She looked up and down. No help, nowhere. All was black. She huddled under a passing Cloud Cover, holding herself together with a huge force of My Will Power and preparing to obliterate. From nothing and nowhere, a downy Comfort Her arrived, along with the voice she knew so well. "You don't have to hunker down and ride it out or evacuate in flight. There's something else now. 'Relax on Impact,' remember?"

With that, the screaming winds diminished and died altogether. She fell with a purpose, away from Impostars. A pale blue butterfly appeared out of nowhere to support her. She focused on the Star, whose familiar blue light enveloped her on contact. ROI Star revealed the presence of EYE M. To her delight, this time she was able to release the butterfly's support and just flow. The butterfly disappeared. She leaned forward and reconnected herself to Perfect Love. EYE Sight replaced My Sight. Her center filled with warmth as she clung to EYE M, shivering violently.

"It was horrible, EYE M! I can hardly believe what just happened. At first it was wonderful. I learned so much from two Seeing EYE Docs. Mind Doc explained why my vision was blocked. Then Body Doc located my intellectual and inner child Earth My Sight problems. They both taught me why I do the things I do and how to let my walls come tumbling down. They had the missing puzzle pieces of my life!"

Perfect Cloud continued, "They said we were a team. They said there was more! I was so excited and all ready to follow. Then…they exploded and disappeared!"

She hovered in the air, shaking with spasms and dripping raindrops, but going nowhere. Her memory caused a physical change. She turned her swollen former Earth My Sight toward EYE M as she waited to hear what He would say.

EYE M held her close as He responded. "You need to know that EYE always have a Plan B. Let's see what happened here. You're an adult. You said you were ready to follow this perfect Star duo, just like Mother and Daddy, the brilliant, shiniest Stars. Forever. This is how you describe a team? Does it sound as if you included yourself as the adult you are today? What's wrong with this picture? First of all, you've met quite a few Impostars. They're doomed to disappear. You created pedestals of many kinds to offer you the security that only comes from Me. The truth is eventually revealed, but often with a price tag of severe pain, wouldn't you agree?"

Perfect Cloud nodded quietly, holding her head down. EYE M's words floated up gently through her Inner EYE M Hear.

"And you've helped them inflate by being quick to increase their worth beyond reality. No Star, not even a great EYE Sight Doc, has the right—or the true and lasting power—to outshine your Create Her. No Co-Star, which in these cases is you, honors Impostars by worshipping them."

EYE M continued, "All three Sight Docs had important messages for you. They were humble and willing, kneeling—not standing—on a podium, not a pedestal. They were balanced too. What about the third Doc? He never exploded. He refused to rise up onto your pedestal. Spirit Doc is His name. He waited to help you find your EYE Space and then to see with EYE M Perfect Vision. You shut Him out by keeping your focus on the others."

"But I couldn't see Him like I could see Body Doc or hear Him like Mind Doc," protested Perfect Cloud. "It seemed like He wasn't important."

"This lesson is major," stated EYE M quietly and firmly. "Spirit Doc is the leader. He's also the one that can only be accessed with a bit of your time and attention. Spirit Doc can assist Mind Doc in correcting faulty thinking. He helps you 'change your mind.' That quiets the emotions that cause Body Doc to work overtime in correcting Dis Ease.

"The body may seem like the cause. It's the biggest, the most visible, and the shiniest. The mind may seem like the second cause. It's the loudest and shines in its own way too. But here's the truth: What you think impacts what you feel, and what you feel impacts either your health or your Dis Ease. Spirit Doc can start you on your perfect path.

It leads directly into EYE M Vision and EYE M Ear. He's the most powerful Seeing EYE Doc!"

She nodded, listening intently.

"If you had allowed Spirit Doc to assist you, you would have had direct access to EYE Sight and EYE M Ear. You would have become Bliss Full, with free-flowing movement, instead of the violent, twisted, circular energy of a HerACane."

Perfect Cloud nodded soberly. "I want to be with *You*, EYE M! How can I show that to You—*now?*"

EYE M watched her. "Remember the figure that created the opening to let you connect to Earth and then quickly disappeared to avoid praise? Spirit Doc is the essence of humility, not humiliation. He allowed others to remove Him from Earth. He didn't disappear, though. After several days He returned. The blue butterfly that appears is not visible to all; when the time was right for you, you could see it. Spirit Doc left a blue light pointing down from My ROI Star. Look through EYE Sight. Meet Spirit Doc. EYE M will speak with you again later."

Perfect Cloud closed her eyes and focused inward. She accessed EYE Space. She finally made the connection between Spirit Doc and EYE M's Single EYE. Spirit Doc was visible now. He asked her some questions about her first love, EYE M. After she nodded and agreed, He brought her down near the waters of the ocean and briefly submerged and cleansed her. He released her, showing her how He could now lift her higher and higher in body, mind, and spirit. Familiar colors spread across the sky.

"EYE M, what do the colors blue, red and pink mean?" Perfect Cloud asked.

"Blue means relax. Your emotional inner child needs a parent for that. Red can be anger, a firm border, passion. The intellectual parent is shown as red. See? Pink is EYE M's Perfect Love. What's been missing for you is Spirit Doc. He serves by bringing you to Me. EYE M is then the real, one and only, Parent of all. See? In your life thus far you've idolized the loud, the big, the bold, and the shiny," He observed.

"Your method for life has been climbing the Earth My Fall Tower to fall into an Impostar's arms, or telling yourself that you are up that high and can rescue them. The result is the same. Pedestals cause a lack of balance and the eventual fall. What goes up must come down."

He continued, "There's good news for you at Power Fall, though. Then you allow EYE M to catch you and have you all to Himself!" He smiled. "EYE M is willing to catch you when you fall, as many times as you wish. Still, it would be a really nice thing—a beautiful thing actually—if you would turn to Me by choice and not from desperation."

Perfect Cloud had to know. "What if I hadn't turned to You? Would You pull me down to Burn Her Pit? I heard that happens." She shuddered. "How cruel."

EYE M replied, while Spirit Doc returned to shine the full force of His light on her. "EYE M never pulls. EYE M waits for you to fall into Me, not into a pit, either by mistake or by design. You appear a bit burned right now, don't you? When you're not seeing through EYE M Vision, just maybe you're placing *yourself* in Burn Her Pit. When you resist Perfect Love, *your* behavior is cruel—cruel to you. For starters, consider your encounters with Freeze Her Burn, Electra Cute Shun, and Acid Rain. Other pitfalls include all forms of Afraid Are and Impostars who try to outshine Me."

He added, "Enablers think they're trying to help. In truth, their efforts interfere with My guidance and your growth by convincing those like you that the burns you sustain aren't real, or that they can cure them for you. Their cushiony cotton wool prevents the consequences that may cause natural pain, which also creates insight that moves you closer to My EYE.

"Don't forget the worst Impostar of all, which happens to be you!" He added. "Your My Will Power obscures EYE Will. My rays provide the warmth and power you seek. Over time you're learning that, aren't you? No, not instant gratification and false bliss from addictions." He paused while she thought this over.

"Now, understand this—you were not made to follow and gaze at ROI Star in awe and wonder. You were made to fall into its warm true light. If you resist true love, you're being cruel to yourself. Then what do you really have to give others? EYE M has all power. EYE M is always nearby, waiting to lift you out of the Impostar Pit. With your permission, of course!"

Perfect Cloud sniffled and nodded.

"Now, about the team concept. When you find another with the same EYE Space access, the two of you will join with equal energy, each parenting yourselves, each following individual and joined passions. Cooperating as a unit, you'll see twice as well. Of course, that's if you choose to use EYE Sight, not My Sight. All you have to do is ask. Sounds too good to be true?"

Perfect Cloud nodded slowly, then shook her head. "I'm beginning to think You can do anything and that I really will like it in the end," she admitted. "How can I more quickly tell the difference between Impostars and real Support Hers?"

EYE M radiated into her center, saturating her with light. He responded as she stretched out in total contentment.

"It's simple but takes a vigilant EYE. Those who are of greatest assistance will deflect any oversized praise you give them and reflect that brilliance back toward Me, and your own perfect self, which is aligned with Me. EYE will be your Instruct Her. Your progress will consist of weakening a bit and downgrading yourself to a slightly lower level." He winked at her. "Sounds backward to you, doesn't it? But then, you're used to listening to Impostars. EYE want to be the only one in your EYE Space. Some call Me jealous, but in truth it's the only way we can really see together. There's a world of weather forms waiting for help and interaction. So let's clean out your EYE Space by releasing any remaining Impostar dust still clinging to your hook. Then we'll remove you, the Co-Star, from their hook! When you're empowered, you'll be all Mine."

"All Yours? What would that look like?" Perfect Cloud asked.

EYE M smiled. "You don't have to know. EYE will show you a little later. But EYE promise you this, it's what you truly want." He re-energized her center.

Perfect Cloud surged forward. In a while, she circled back again. "EYE M," she mused, "I used to think Mother Cloud and Daddy Double HimACane were good parents—great, in fact. But after the Seeing EYE Docs showed me all the IMPs floating in my Earth My Sight, better known as family-of-origin blocks, and all the impacts of repeating those, it seems like they were actually bad. I don't see how they could have done their best."

She continued, "In fact, much of what they did looks like their worst. I don't know how I can forgive that. The adult in me thinks it's a mistake to let them off the hook. The emotional part of me feels cheated and betrayed and wishes she had never trusted either of them in the first place. It's like I was taught all the wrong things from the ones who were supposed to teach me all about life. I tried hard too! It's as if I got all A's—in the wrong school! But now it's too late. My parents are gone."

"That's understandable," validated EYE M. "Looking through your Earth My Sight displays that vision. Even when properly parenting yourself, you might come to the same conclusions. However, if you choose to look at each of your parents through EYE Space, inviting EYE M to rerun the old movie, you might see a different story. It's all about perspective. The perspective screen is a final P.S. Though the positive or negative impacts are real, there's an explanation for all behaviors. That final explanation, also known as reframing, leads to authentic forgiveness. And by the way," He added quietly but intently, "I'm in charge of that final piece. Are you willing to watch?"

Perfect Cloud agreed, intrigued. Deep red curtains opened to reveal a perspective screen. The skylights dimmed. As she watched, EYE M showed her Mother Cloud's key experiences.

"When Mother Cloud was younger, she often said no to new life experiences, mainly out of fear. Her parents supported the problem instead of the solution, also known as enabling. They didn't insist that she do chores, learn to drive, finish her studies, or learn to support herself. They didn't help her to make a correction when she made a mistake. 'Tough love' is only tough on those enforcing boundaries and holding loved ones accountable. It's not tough on the loved one. Instead, Mother learned to expect one of two outcomes: either perfection or the perceived humiliation of rejection. She had a bright mind but didn't learn the necessary steps for growth in that area. Afraid Are increased."

A picture revealed Mother Cloud raining. She held the rain in and eventually it froze.

"As a result, her only hope for freedom became the good will of a Power Full Him. Catching a Double HimACane required Storm Attraction. This was also known in her world as S.A. The catch also required a decorated hook. She became a Co-Star of the Storm Attracted, also known as a Storm Object. You were trained to follow suit. Two dancers depending on each other as parent and child instead of as two adults can't express EYE Motion. Their dance is...? Fill in the blank, Perfect Cloud."

"Tox Sick!" Perfect Cloud beamed up at Him, strangely pleased. "EYE M, why didn't her parents insist she empower herself? Didn't they care about her? They weren't good parents. In fact, they were bad, right?"

EYE M moved closer. "Don't you see the pattern yet? You're still looking through your own My Sight. Why not do something different now? Watch an EYE Space review of Mother Cloud's own Mother Cloud."

The perspective screen revealed a woman giving birth to Mother Cloud very shortly after a Commit Meant to her chosen HimACane. She had several more Little Clouds and became too busy and unable to hold boundaries with them all.

"When your Mother Cloud said no to growing experiences, her mother allowed that. She simply turned to the other Little Clouds without realizing the eventual impact on Mother's self-esteem and abilities. Mother Cloud's daddy handed her sweets if she had any feelings, just like he gave himself…and just like she gave to you, Perfect Cloud. And so it goes," observed EYE M. "The Ice Age began when your Mother Cloud was very little. She did give you her best. She tried with what she had. Do you need to see more? Your mother's mother's mother, perhaps?"

"No, I see now, EYE M. I've never looked at this through Your vision. What about Daddy Double HimACane?"

"Let me present the next Double Feature," announced EYE M. On the screen He showed her the life of the young Daddy Double HimACane.

"Daddy Double HimACane's own daddy was simply named Cloud. He worked all night and slept all day. In his absence, Daddy tried to be the Special Him, a rescuer, even a mate for his mother! His feelings came out in music. He was afraid to let the music out of the Box, though, because without those Boxed Borders, he might somehow not do it well enough. He thought he would fail. He decided that whirling around to collect Debris Resources for women was the answer. When he discovered Toxic Rain, he thought he had a double answer. He inhaled quite a few Dust Devil Tubes too. But none of them worked out in the end. He ended up disrespecting Mother Cloud for the same reasons he was attracted to her. She resented the situation in which she originally felt secure."

EYE M narrated as the pictures rolled. "Your daddy sent his mother stirred-up Debris Resources to make her happy. She responded by sending them all back to him with a different bow, as a gift in return. You see, the joy of gifts is in the giving. She didn't want Resources from her son or from anyone else in order to feel more happiness. What she really wanted was a relationship with her absent husband. He made a living but not a life."

He continued, "Fast forward now. Your Mother Cloud also became upset with Daddy's Toxic Rain use while allowing and even supplying this liquid. This, Perfect Cloud, is called Co-Depend Dance. It takes two to dance, remember. Mother took in too many sweets in response to Daddy's withdrawal from their relationship and to his over-attachment to you, his daughter. She became larger and larger and less attractive both to herself and to him as a result."

Perfect Cloud listened and frowned. The movie paused.

"You, Perfect Cloud, thought Daddy was wonderful, no matter what he did. Daddy Double HimACane basked in the starlit worship of one who was easily impressed. Of course it felt good to him. He didn't realize it, but the inappropriate nature of 'dating' his own daughter would entangle you later."

EYE M continued, "And your daddy's daddy was a twin, and he—"

"It's okay, EYE M," interjected Perfect Cloud. "I truly am following You now."

"So do you need to see Dim Double Ex's earlier life? Believe me, there are reasons for his learned behavior too."

"No," Perfect Cloud answered thoughtfully. "I think I know. I don't like it, but I understand it. I'm beginning to realize that we took turns as predator and prey, parent and child, a real Co-Depend Dance."

"Yes, it was. I think you're remembering the goal now. When your childhood suitcase is finally cleaned out well, you're able to leave childhood behind. You can become an empowered adult who relies on your one unconditional love. If both mates are fully dependent on Me, it's the foundation for true, interdependent, adult love."

"I'm ready to forgive everyone now, as best I can. Please help me." Perfect Cloud's voice was small but steady.

"That's real progress," EYE M commended her. "Let's start with the hardest one. Are you ready to forgive yourself? Are you ready to look at and listen to your own behavior through EYE M Vision and EYE M Hear? I know you sorted through the ways you affected your Young Clouds while you climbed the Steps Ladder and while working with the Seeing EYE Docs. I was there, you know."

"Yes, EYE M, and I amended where I could. I'm correcting and making progress toward living an entirely different kind of life now. You showed me a new way. But I've had a very hard time forgiving myself. I so much wish I could undo the past. I don't want to regret the past. I need to see and hear this through your EYE M Vision and EYE M Hear so I can move forward."

"Perfect Cloud," stated EYE M, "your fear of traveling on your own, of finishing studies, and of providing your own Resources come from Mother Cloud. Your fear of becoming Power Full was also from Mother Cloud, whose Afraid Are increased as she felt competitive with her own daughter. Daddy alternately supported or discouraged these disempowerment processes, which was confusing for you.

"Daddy Double HimACane gave you a message of passion, color, and excitement that crossed personal boundaries and separated you from a relationship with Mother Cloud. You trusted that he always 'had your back.' But at a critical time in your life, Daddy's fear of displeasing Mother Cloud caused him to sabotage you when you tried to become authentic."

EYE M continued, "Even the very personal and individual expression of your choice of music was forced on you in parental fashion through Daddy and Mother. You worshipped them as Impostars long after the time had come for them to redirect you to your real Star, also known as ROI.

"Perfect Cloud, when you found Toxic Rain, you thought you had found Courage Us. You believed that your My Will Power could make you a wonderful mother and mate. After a while, terrified, you couldn't stop soaking up Toxic Rain even when you wanted to. You had never named or really felt a true feeling. Lack of emotional skills coupled with Co-Depend Dance and Toxic Rain pain almost ended your life. It did cost you the respect of others and, worst of all, your own self-respect. And, yes, when you were a young adult, Mother and Daddy felt frightened, concerned, and impacted by your addiction too. That's your part in any resentment toward them."

He spoke in a kind but direct manner that Perfect Cloud recognized as EYE M Perfect Love once again.

"Is it too late now to start over?" Perfect Cloud's voice was even smaller. "With all You've taught me I could be a really good Mother Cloud to my babies. I want them to remember You and know You. They deserve to feel Bliss Full. They're bigger now, though. What can we do?"

"Your surrender and willingness were honest when the time was right," consoled EYE M, as Perfect Cloud rained and rained in a deluge. "Now it's time to move forward."

Chapter 12

Free Flow

EYE M summarizes the stages needed for adult empowerment. He describes the freedom from Earth Impostars and how to achieve detachment and increased EYE Sight. EYE M reminds her of the importance of leaving negative childhood impacts behind and supports her in forgiving herself and others. He teaches her ways to be of service to others while near, but not overly attached to, Earth. He explains the conditions for finding a healthy mate in the future. He reminds her of the importance of three main relationships in a specific order. Surprises are revealed.

Freedom is the goal." EYE M's voice seemed to fill her heart. "Freedom is your choice to rise up toward Me, Perfect Love, even while you're still near Earth. To become free an adult first needs to disconnect from

Earthly childhood. This needs to happen as soon as possible, when the time is right. That newly empowered parent can bring the inner child and fully come to Me. EYE M freedom.

"When you're an adult but still holding onto and repeating the painful memories of your childhood, you're trapped there. It's the first relationship addiction. Fear, false shame, and anger are strong bonds to the past. All children think their parents are Perfect Love. They repeat the bargaining stage of grief. 'Maybe if I try again childhood will turn out differently. I must not have earned Perfect Love from them or they would have given it to me. I caused it, so now I have to cure it.' It's difficult to disconnect from childhood parents known as Imperfect Love and move closer to Perfect Love without balance."

"Then how do I find that balance to move forward?" asked Perfect Cloud, shaking her head as her raindrops slowed.

EYE M smiled. "Identifying not only the negative impacts of each parent but also the positive ones provides the release. Empowered adults then find healthy boundaries for themselves. They won't continue seeking their 'other half.' The result? They can then serve others with the right motives. They won't seek either power or approval—both of which are known as codependency. Relationship addiction will lessen or leave altogether. There will be total emotional dependence on Me. Freedom."

"Okay," agreed Perfect Cloud. She tightened her lips in thought, then gave a huge grin. She remembered: Wherever she went, EYE M was all around her. His fleecy warmth conveyed a love force so large she couldn't see past it and didn't want to try. He knew where she wanted to go even when she didn't know for sure herself!

"Yes, my Daddy Double Him reminded me of You in some important ways," Perfect Cloud said. "He exposed me to music. When he played his Boxed Music I remembered my inner love for that and for variations from other styles. Daddy taught me to love adventure, even though it was from far away. He modeled enthusiasm. I have a lot of it now too. He caught me every time I slid down from the My Fall Tower. I felt safe and secure and loved, just like I always do with You.

"And Mother Cloud taught me how to look attractive and to behave properly with others. She taught me to read and spell and to speak another language. She taught me to tell interesting and funny stories and to laugh. Laughing reminds me of You a lot."

EYE M nodded, smiling. "It's time to bring forward those positive impacts—purposely—as the gifts they were in your childhood. The negative ones need reframing and My forgiveness. Some childhood cords will automatically release, while others will be worn away by fraying a bit at a time. When Imperfect Love is released you can access your own adult with the child. Together you're free to join your one true Parent: Me! EYE M Perfect Love. The blue light from the butterfly is always available and willing to bring you back toward your true home when you 'Relax on Impact.'"

Perfect Cloud's form became stiff. "But if I leave my childhood home behind to become my own new adult parent, then I'm not honoring my Earthly parents, am I? I thought You said I should honor them?"

"Yes, I did, Perfect Cloud. The Earthly child must honor the parents by obeying them. Honoring your Earthly mother and father when you become adult, however, means becoming the most empowered and complete version of yourself possible. Worshipping childhood parents as an adult? No, those Earthly parents, properly known as Imperfect Love, lead the child's way and hopefully teach the child to fly when adulthood arrives.

"The problem? Over compliance or defiance in childhood is a trap that continues the emotional process of childhood long into adulthood. That leaves Me out. As a healthy adult you visit your childhood parents with interdependence, not obedience. You show respect, connect to others' emotions, and yet have thoughts and boundaries of your own. Freedom for you is obeying Me and My Will for your life.

"One day," He continued, "your Young Clouds will also view their parents' impacts, both the positives and negatives. And so it goes. Now do you see why only EYE M is capable of seeing the bigger picture? If it were left up to others, compassion would be absent. When your Earth life ends you'll undergo a transition inventory. If you invite Me in, EYE will support you with unconditional love while you review all of your Earth actions. You'll feel the positive and negative feelings those behaviors caused in others.

"Heaven or hell? Didn't you experience what seemed to be both with Impostar love, substances, Resources, and Power? If EYE M with you it's all about learning. And let's get one thing straight: There is no 'obliteration,' but rather 'transformation.' The only thing that will obliterate is the illusion that you were ever really anything but Perfect Cloud, through and through."

He added, with a chuckle, "EYE M EYE Sight. EYE see through the clouds. Let My sun shine through this flood now or we'll both have to swim!" He winked as Perfect Cloud hiccupped.

"Just so you know, those parents of yours still care and are nearby to be of help in a new way. Look." He pointed up and out. "The real lesson here as a grown Cloud is to find and release childhood negatives. Next, find and repeat the positives. Then we have generational blessings instead of teaching generational mistakes. Now, about your Little Clouds? Leave your children's futures to Me. EYE M capable!"

EYE M smiled. So did Perfect Cloud, right through her raindrops.

He continued. "Work to stay right-sized. Not too big, not too small. EYE Sight focuses on that. When you're given opportunities to serve, you're accountable for keeping your EYE Space clear and taking time out to hear My Voice. EYE M your Direct Her. EYE M doesn't recommend shameless personal promotion. EYE do, however, suggest that you go forward whenever possible, supporting others with what you've learned.

"EYE M's will for you is to educate, to confront and to comfort those EYE bring to you. Give as you have received. Now that you know how to access EYE Space, this is how you will look when you choose to use it in the future. This symbolizes you as your own parent, outlined in clear red boundaries. It means your inner child, in blue, is heard, protected, and understood. And directing this Free Flow is EYE M, with a Single EYE, located—"

Perfect Cloud jumped in with the open enthusiasm of her true inner child. "It's the letter 'I' only with You at the top! It's the EYE of a HerACane! The place of perfect peace. It's Your EYE, right? Your Single EYE! What does the pink glow all around it mean?"

EYE M nodded, smiling but serious. "EYE M serenity. EYE M perfect peace. EYE M always available to you. The pink glow reflects the joy you experienced with Me when it was just the two of us at the very beginning. Your entire life is once again surrounded with sweet pink cotton EYE candy, My love that never leaves."

Perfect Cloud applauded. "I love that. What is the white form in the very center of Your EYE?"

"Look closely," urged EYE M. "It's the white bird you always wished for."

Perfect Cloud clapped. "I can fly like that seagull now! I'm free too!"

"Look more closely," EYE M suggested. "That gull, when it's seen through My EYE, can also be viewed as a white dove—a symbol of peace."

"Wow, yes! One more thing I have to know—why am I called Perfect Cloud only when I'm with You?"

"EYE M really glad to finally answer that question," He said. "Perfect Cloud is who you always are. It's who you always were. It's who all the others are too! It's only possible to see perfection through Me. When EYE M here, you're less distracted and more likely to look through My Vision."

He looked into her eyes. "Through Earth My Sights, perfection comes and goes. Have you heard of hero one day, zero the next? The Earth goal is to achieve awareness and insight and to learn to make corrections. Perfection and Earth vision don't usually match, at least not in Earth terms! That's another illusion. The glare causes twisted vision. Seeing It Near is also called S.I.N. Missing the mark. Detachment is needed!"

"That's another thing, EYE M," added Perfect Cloud. "Why did You leave me in the beginning? Where do You go when I leave to follow Earth My Sight?"

EYE M pointed behind her. "EYE M always here. You left Me, or thought you did! You thought you had separated from Me forever, didn't you? I let you have your own My Will. You thought you detached from Me and then were all alone, but here's the truth: We're connected. Always.

In all ways. Turn around and look. I've always 'had your back.'"

Perfect Cloud turned, straining to see. Attached to the middle of her back hung a cord that held her snugly to EYE M and disappeared from view into the endless sky. Her mouth opened wide as she stared at the security of Perfect Love she thought she had unhooked from a long time ago.

"It's in your Blind Spot," said EYE M, smiling.

"That's always been here?" she exclaimed. "And I never knew EYE M had a sense of humor!"

"When your My Sight is blind, of course EYE M able to see," He said. "EYE M sees from deep within your center. That cord passes through your back all the way into your heart. When your Earth Ears are closed, of course EYE M Hear can also open. But as EYE said, EYE never pull. When you decide you prefer EYE Will over your My Will Power, then you'll travel with Me instead of on your own. It's truly the way to fly! I call it 'Flow.'

"For the record, EYE don't have a sense of humor, but rather EYE M a sense of humor—and quite a few other things! Remember when you thought you left Me for those shiny Impostars that I told you were empty? You were so eager to explore on your own. Yes, they appear flashy—more than EYE M. Now you know they're truly empty. But here's a surprise: They're also connected to Me. When they're filled with Me, their purpose is clear. It's a full circle,

Perfect Cloud. Everyone and everything returns to Me. All are a part of Me. They just haven't turned around to check. Take a look now through EYE M Vision."

As EYE M spoke, Perfect Cloud marveled at the connection between EYE M and everyone and everything. When they were filled with EYE M's love, they filled with pink and purpose. She climbed the EYE FALL Tower and slid down into Perfect Love, emerging with EYE M in her center.

She fell, fell in love with EYE M. She awakened from a deep, deep sleep.

"Will You stay within me like this, EYE M? Even though I'm still floating near Earth?"

"Absolutely," He replied. "You were meant to commit to ME. That's your first Commit Meant. For now, your true mission is to navigate near Earth while focusing on My Single EYE. Others will be drawn to your light when your focus is on Me. EYE M Vision shines through you."

"Oh! And why do I sometimes cry as I reconnect to You in my center, EYE M?" She had to know. "I should be happy, not sad then, right?"

He nodded. "Each time you lean into acceptance of that which is truly over—childhood and Impostar security—your Earth Vision breaks open. Acceptance is the final stage of grief. You might feel empty and disillusioned, until EYE Will lift you higher than you could possibly ever rise by yourself.

"Be aware, though," He cautioned, "that each time you lean into EYE Will while you're still attached to Earth, the Impostars Rebound follows. You've stretched toward Me. Suddenly you're snapped backward. This creates an intense contrast. The Impostars can be blinding and overwhelming. S.I.N. is truly 'seeing it near'— seeing the Impostars too near. Remember, Relax on Impact. Don't react this time by efforts to 'power up against them' or try to charm them. Those behaviors increase your Earth Vision. Don't return to the childhood Imperfect Love of parents or others with either compliance or defiance."

"Hmm. Could that also be called de-pliance?" suggested Perfect Cloud, laughing.

"Sure it could." EYE M drew her new word in the sky with clouds and laughed too, creating a sky celebration that twirled her around and around.

"Wow, I didn't know You could laugh so hard!" Perfect Cloud felt amazed.

"Of course EYE can laugh," EYE M continued. "EYE created laughing! Stretch toward Me for a while, until you feel more comfortable connected to Me than you do to Earth. Leave behind the My Rose-Colored glasses you wore to deal with Imperfect Love. Release the need to become a force. That is using your My Will. EYE Will supply all the Earth Debris Resources you need to be comfortable and of service while near Earth. Relax and refocus on Me. Bit by bit, you'll detach from Earth into Me. My Perfect Vision will be your new normal!"

"Release MY Will?" Perfect Cloud looked concerned. "Then I shouldn't *try* to do anything at all? I should just fly? Is that called winging it?"

EYE M smiled and nodded. "Your efforts are necessary, but your My Will blocks EYE Will. Leave the outcomes to Me. That's the difference. Bring your newly parented inner child to Me. Obey Me, Perfect Love.

You'll become the Free Flow. You'll view Earth with compassion and take necessary action, but with true detachment. The remaining Earth cords will fray or release with the others. True freedom is living in My Will for you. Perfect Love creates the power and bliss that you've always sought. One glorious day you'll be set free altogether. For now, you have a journey near Earth, and this time it's with a mission. You'll learn to move with Free Flow.

"In order of importance," EYE M summarized, "the three relationships in your life are not with Power, Resources, and So Much More Love on Earth. They're first with EYE M, second with yourself, and last with all others."

Perfect Cloud took it all in, then frowned. "I thought others came before me."

"You can only give away what you first have for yourself," He explained. "Loving yourself is wholeness, not selfishness. It comes only from My Perfect Love. Now look at the bigger picture, further away from Earth Vision and through EYE Vision. Look again at the Her Cloud who 'took your place' with your Dim Double Ex. She did in fact take your place. Look through My EYE."

She gasped at the new view of the Hidden Her Cloud, now having trouble moving on her own. Perfect Cloud felt sad, compassionate, even grateful. She felt a surge of forgiveness.

"You had a Hidden Him of your own too, remember?"

Perfect Cloud nodded at EYE M's insightful comment, her head lowered.

EYE M moved even closer to her as He explained, "I know you felt victimized by your Dim Double Ex. Here's the truth: Children can be victimized. When childhood's over, Perfect Cloud, all have power of choice unless they're ill or very old. Seeing EYE Docs are always available. Therefore, there are no predators or prey. There are simply two adults who have unresolved pain from distorted vision.

Your own Earth Vision has been a bit cloudy and confused in the past too, wouldn't you agree?"

He continued. "There's only one difference between you and Dim Double Ex, who in reality is also called Perfect Cloud, and between you and Hidden Her, who in reality is also called Perfect Cloud too. That difference is that *you* had what's known as a breakdown. Then a break*through* occurred. You were willing to climb a Steps Ladder, to work with Seeing EYE Docs, and to learn new skills. You returned to where you left off with studies—*not* to Storm Sanctuary or Storm Surge Lead Her Ship Study, but rather to Free Flow Cloud Academy. And, yes, you learned numbers!"

They both clapped.

"It's time to let Me forgive the others for past mistakes. Release them to fly free. Bring yourself to Me for forgiveness, too. You move forward with Me," He directed her.

Perfect Cloud smiled at Him and tried out her movement now. She was able to fly with EYE M *and* on her own at last. They were a team. Her various passions altered the shades of her breezes. Like the seagull, she flapped her feathered layers for movement and definition. Like a butterfly, her delicate edges fluttered softly. EYE M's Eagle EYE had replaced Afraid Are.

EYE M Perfect Vision filled her. Together they traveled over mountains and hillsides. Perfect Cloud gasped with joy as they flew alongside the seagull she had thought obliterated a long time ago. It was not only alive but transformed into a new bird—a dove! She and the dove flowed side by side.

Perfect Cloud, still filled with EYE M Vision and EYE M Hear, asked if she could travel distances now to share what she had learned. "I'm new at this. What should I say to those I meet? How can I support them without enabling them or rejecting them?" she implored EYE M.

"You don't need to be perfect to be inspirational," He said. "You do need to be authentic and humble. This takes not only education but also practice. Review the Seeing EYE Docs' messages. If you stay on the Steps Ladder journey, that will help you, too. Move closer to Earth now and let's practice the contrast. The Impostars will surround you. Let them. Relax on Impact. Then stretch away toward Me. Return several times. Earth IMPs will surround you less each time you visit without wearing My Rose-Colored glasses. Go ahead."

Perfect Cloud did as she was told. EYE M, of course, predicted these outcomes perfectly. When she had finished this practice she was filled with a new awareness.

"EYE M, when Your vision and hearing are within me, somehow this isn't quite as hard. I don't feel as scared. Maybe a little, but not a lot." She smiled.

He nodded. "Exactly. That exercise develops true Detach Meant. Remember, right now you have Earth My Sight unless you choose to turn to Me for clear EYE Space! Listen with your EYE M Hear for My Voice. Mistakes happen while traveling near Earth. When you need to make a correction, just ask for help through humility. No shame, no pride. Look for the butterfly and lean into the light, my ROI Star. You'll know you've let Me into your center when your Earth world seems quite a bit smaller than My Single EYE."

"EYE M, if only this freedom of form and feelings could stay! Will everything I've found leave again if I pick the wrong mate? When will I be able to have a healthy mate relationship? What are the right conditions? How will I know, EYE M, when my mate arrives?" Perfect Cloud, of course, had to know all these things. "There have been so many Him Clouds, Him Storms, and HimACanes." She shook her head.

"Perfect Cloud, you're ready for a mate when you don't really need one, but you want one—when you and EYE are a solid unit, a Star of our own, in fact. When EYE M Number One to saturate your heart, then you're able to achieve Independ Dance. Your happiness lies in total Depend Dance on Me. Yes, I love the words you blend together, your special words! After all, EYE created words!"

EYE M leaned even closer to Perfect Cloud, filling her with warmth and trust. He continued, "The next dance, Inter Depend Dance, is with your mate. That means each of you is equally empowered but chooses to share. When two of you overlap to view situations through shared EYE Space, Perfect Vision is magnified. It's clearer for the couple and for each as an individual too.

"Your ideal mate will look a lot like you in ways that count: parented inner child with willingness for EYE M Vision and EYE M Hear at the top. Your mate will be committed and willing to make emotional connection without losing individuality and focus. Earth life is mainly about corrections and movement. You and your mate will support each other's dreams. You'll each hear your own music. The healthiest mates will support one another instead of trying to control the other, as if parent and child."

He turned away from her and toward the skies, now dotted with a variety of clouds and storms. They all moved in closer as He spoke:

"For my friends—all who have EYE Space to see and EYE M Hear Space to hear: Never forget, EYE M your Number One. ROI, Relax on Impact, is My Star," He summarized. "My Star can also be called ROI, Return on Investment, the real—*the only real*—investment in your life. EYE M also known as El Roi, the God Who Sees.

"You have free will. EYE hold you in the palm of My Hand. EYE M waiting. My Single EYE patiently waits to enter. To some my EYE appears brown. To others it seems blue, and to others it appears green. EYE M all colors.

"When you relax and release your My Will, EYE Will become your powerful center. Live, love, and work on Earth until you transform. But true

power is not there. Don't attach. If you do, you're hooked to the largest and brightest Impostar of all.

"Unhook and then detach, starting with childhood. Ask Seeing EYE Docs or others for help in unpacking your childhood suitcase. Find closure!" He looked at Perfect Cloud and smiled. "Close your childhood suitcase!"

They both laughed.

"How? By bringing forward the positive impacts from each parent as the childhood gifts they are. By releasing the negative impacts through My reframing EYE. By reparenting your inner child with healthy boundaries. Finally, by bringing that transformed, reparented child to Me. EYE Will forgive all—parents, Impostars, and you. Release the need to see, to hear, or to know anything totally on your own.

"When your My Sight is empty, EYE can see for you. EYE M Vision. When your Earth Ear is empty, EYE can hear for you. EYE M Ear. EYE Will flow you to your Purpose with passion and energy. Perfect and peaceful, warm and protected, loved and safe, forever and ever... Free Flow...Bliss Full."

Perfect Cloud gasped with delight as EYE M turned back toward her, swooped her up, and lifted her high. "EYE know how much you love music, Perfect Cloud. Especially for you, EYE Will provide a Music All mate whose notes are inside *and* outside of the Box! He'll appreciate you as the ideal audience!"

"And You'll be our guidance, also called our God Dance!" she clapped. "Or I can dance to music alone with You! Just You and me!" And together, they danced. Others danced too.

"Do you remember Bliss Full now?" EYE M smiled. "Emotionally open, perfectly parented, guided by My single EYE, relaxed and saturated with My unconditional love?"

Now Perfect Cloud remembered. EYE M knew her in all ways, inside and out. He had a perfect plan made just for her life called EYE

Will. Saturated and secure, Perfect Cloud sang songs radiating from her full, satisfied heart and moved with uninhibited joy to the rhythm of her pulsing inner beat—her very own drums!

"I didn't earn back the name 'Perfect' from the Impostars, but I did earn it back from You, EYE M, didn't I?" asked Perfect Cloud.

"You didn't have to earn it at all," He corrected. "It's always been your name. The name 'Perfect' only disappeared through an illusion. Seeing It Near is from Impostar glare. Keep your distance! Become dis-illusioned!" He tilted toward her to emphasize the point. She nodded with a serious face.

Then she squealed with surprise and delight as she suddenly heard the arrival of Mother Cloud's harp music—for the first time! It sounded perfectly imperfect. Then Daddy's formerly Boxed Music returned, joining Mother's music with a new passion. Another surprise: Daddy followed Mother Cloud's lead! Then they played their individual music together.

Perfect Cloud clapped at their efforts. As she waved goodbye and turned fully toward EYE M, in the distance she heard the return of EYE M's theme song. EYE M smiled and nodded to a Perfect Him Cloud waiting patiently behind Him. He carried many musical instruments both inside and outside of the Box. Perfect Cloud smiled from the inside out. With EYE M between them, they shared the special song. The music increased…and became dimensional.

"You knew me! And You *know* me!" sang the two Perfect Clouds with EYE M. Others joined in.

END

On a final note: I'd like to share with you an event that occurred two years ago while working on the audiovisual version of this book. As we focused on Chapter 12, when Perfect Cloud was about to learn the process of deep forgiveness, Aaron Arnold of FeatherDot Productions suggested I locate a picture of a bird of prey that he could use to symbolize her perceived life predators.

On my way home several days later, I noticed a large bird under a tree right across from my office. It was just sitting, and didn't move, even as I cautiously left my car and approached it with my phone camera. It was clearly blind, with a film covering its eyes. I hadn't had time to even begin the search when God's Perfect Timing revealed to me a bird of prey! I reported it to Orlando Animal Control, who transferred the bird to the Audubon Center for Birds of Prey in Maitland, Florida. I followed this Red Shouldered Hawk's rehabilitation through the services of the dedicated workers who appeared.

An amazing volunteer named Janice Buczkowski supported me in the joint release of this gorgeous bird while Aaron Arnold captured the event on film. That hawk "was blind, but now it sees"...and flies.

About the Author

I'm Jill Haire, a Licensed Mental Health Counselor, National Certified Counselor, and Certified Addictions Professional. My private practice,

Free Flow Counseling, is located in Southwest Orlando. As a mental health counselor, I provide support along with education to guide individuals, couples, and families in learning communications skills and practicing healthy boundaries. As a former hospice counselor, I assist those recovering from various types of grief. As an addictions professional, I offer emotional literacy and communication skills that support dimensional 12-Step recovery. I also combine these skills and knowledge into deeper psychotherapy to process family-of-origin issues. When left unresolved, these issues impact individuals long past the end of childhood, creating *relationship addiction.*

Free Flow Consulting has emerged to produce the book you're holding in your hands—*Relax on Impact*—in both written and audiovisual formats. The *audiovisual version of*Relax on Impact* is a twelve-chapter, six-hour production with soundtrack, curriculum, questions, and topics for various audiences and with licensure packages. The book's purpose is to entertain, educate, and inspire all who seek empowerment and freedom in becoming authentic.

Very few family systems or schools teach skills such as anger management, emotional literacy, or healthy personal boundaries and growth.

We need to learn to "check in" rather than to "check out" from life using these skills.

While some of us don't suffer from substance abuse or other obvious addictions, many, I think, can relate to addictive behaviors of other kinds. Underneath the surface addictions lies 'relationship addiction,' probably the most powerful of them all. As a mental health counselor, a grief counselor and an addictions professional, I believe that relationships create problems for many of us – not only relationships with our mates and friends, but with ourselves. That's where it all begins.

It's become horrifyingly clear that our entire world needs training to release the power struggle and to learn connection and communication that lies beneath the anger wall. That work begins with the individual. It actually begins in childhood. It's my passionate hope that one day this knowledge and new behavior will interrupt existing and generational dysfunction.

Many of us seek the inward peace from forgiving others, the empowerment from releasing ourselves as victims, the self forgiveness from harming others. This all leads to our final dependency on the one true Star, our Higher Power. I refer to this state as the Free Flow.

*On a cautionary note, family of origin work is called "psychotherapy," and isn't self-help. Portions of this are suggested in the book, and this needs to be supervised by a licensed counselor.

Resources

Chapters 10, 11, and 12

Charles L. Whitfield, Healing the Child Within
(Deerfield Beach, Fl. Health Communications, 1987)

Robert Hemfelt, Frank Minith, Paul Meier, Love Is A Choice
(Nashvillle, Tennnessee Thomas Nelson, Inc. 1989)

Corey, Gerald, Theory and Practice of Psychotherapy, Sixth Edition,
(Wadsworth Brooks/ Cole Counseling, Imprint of Wadsworth, a
division of Thomson Learning, 2001)

Ellis, A. (1991). Reason and Emotion in Psychotherapy
(New York: Carol.)

Ellis, A. (1993). Reflections on Rational Emotive Therapy.
(Journal of Consulting and Clinical Psychology, 61. 199-201.)

Ellis, A. & Dryden, W. (1997). The Practice of Rational Emotive
Behavior Therapy.
(New York: Springer Publishing Company, Inc.)

A free eBook edition is available with the purchase of this book.

To claim your free eBook edition:

1. Download the Shelfie app.
2. Write your name in upper case in the box.
3. Use the Shelfie app to submit a photo.
4. Download your eBook to any device.

Shelfie

A *free* eBook edition is available
with the purchase of this print book.

CLEARLY PRINT YOUR NAME ABOVE IN UPPER CASE

Instructions to claim your free eBook edition:
1. Download the Shelfie app for Android or iOS
2. Write your name in **UPPER CASE** above
3. Use the Shelfie app to submit a photo
4. Download your eBook to any device

Print & Digital Together Forever.

Snap a photo   Free eBook   Read anywhere

The Morgan James
Speakers Group

We connect Morgan James published
authors with live and online events
and audiences whom will benefit
from their expertise.

Morgan James makes all of our titles available
through the Library for All Charity Organizations.

www.LibraryForAll.org